Oscar Fingal O'Flahertie Wills Wilde (16 October 1854 – 30 November 1900) was an Irish poet and playwright. After writing in different forms throughout the 1880s, he became one of London's most popular playwrights in the early 1890s. He is best remembered for his epigrams and plays, his novel The Picture of Dorian Gray, and the circumstances of his criminal conviction for homosexuality, imprisonment, and early death at age 46. Wilde's parents were successful Anglo-Irish intellectuals in Dublin. Their son became fluent in French and German early in life. At university, Wilde read Greats; he proved himself to be an outstanding classicist, first at Trinity College Dublin, then at Oxford. He became known for his involvement in the rising philosophy of aestheticism, led by two of his tutors, Walter Pater and John Ruskin. After university, Wilde moved to London into fashionable cultural and social circles. (Source: Wikipedia)

Literary works:
Ravenna (1878)
Poems (1881)
The Happy Prince and Other Stories (1888)
Lord Arthur Savile's Crime and Other Stories (1891)
A House of Pomegranates (1891)
Intentions (1891)
The Picture of Dorian Gray (1890)
The Soul of Man under Socialism (1891)
Lady Windermere's Fan (1892)
A Woman of No Importance (1893)
An Ideal Husband (1898)
The Importance of Being Earnest (1898)
De Profundis (1905)
The Ballad of Reading Gaol (1898)
The Portrait of Mr. W. H. (1889)

AN IDEAL HUSBAND,

CHARMIDES
AND OTHER POEMS
&
CHILDREN IN PRISON
AND OTHER CRUELTIES OF PRISON LIFE

OSCAR WILDE

PRINCE CLASSICS

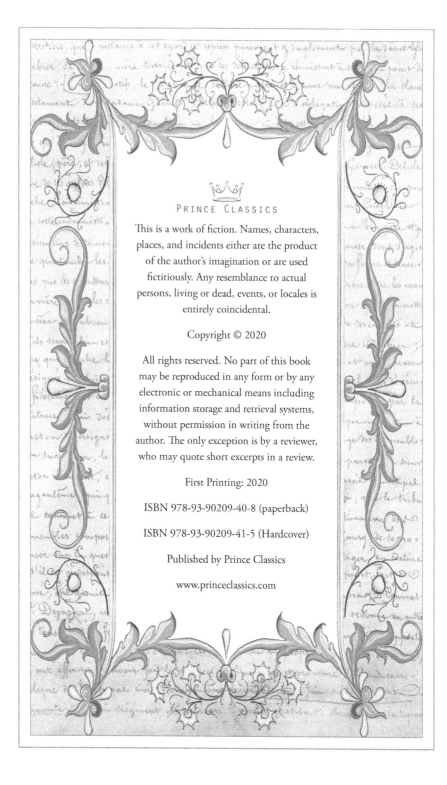

PRINCE CLASSICS

Copyright © 2020

First Printing: 2020

ISBN 978-93-90209-40-8 (paperback)

ISBN 978-93-90209-41-5 (Hardcover)

Published by Prince Classics

www.princeclassics.com

Contents

AN IDEAL HUSBAND.

CHARMIDES
AND OTHER POEMS
&
CHILDREN IN PRISON
AND OTHER CRUELTIES OF PRISON LIFE

AN IDEAL HUSBAND

THE PERSONS OF THE PLAY

THE EARL OF CAVERSHAM, K.G.

VISCOUNT GORING, his Son

SIR ROBERT CHILTERN, Bart., Under-Secretary for Foreign Affairs

VICOMTE DE NANJAC, Attaché at the French Embassy in London

MR. MONTFORD

MASON, Butler to Sir Robert Chiltern

PHIPPS, Lord Goring's Servant

JAMES   }

HAROLD } Footmen

LADY CHILTERN

LADY MARKBY

THE COUNTESS OF BASILDON

MRS. MARCHMONT

MISS MABEL CHILTERN, Sir Robert Chiltern's Sister

MRS. CHEVELEY

THE SCENES OF THE PLAY

Act I. *The Octagon Room in Sir Robert Chiltern's House in Grosvenor Square.*

Act II. *Morning-room in Sir Robert Chiltern's House.*

Act III. *The Library of Lord Goring's House in Curzon Street.*

Act IV. *Same as Act II.*

Time: *The Present*

Place: *London.*

The action of the play is completed within twenty-four hours.

THEATRE ROYAL, HAYMARKET

Sole Lessee: Mr. Herbert Beerbohm Tree

Managers: Mr. Lewis Waller and Mr. H. H. Morell

January 3rd, 1895

The Earl of Caversham	*Mr. Alfred Bishop.*
Viscount Goring	*Mr. Charles H. Hawtrey.*
Sir Robert Chiltern	*Mr. Lewis Waller.*
Vicomte de Nanjac	*Mr. Cosmo Stuart.*
Mr. Montford	*Mr. Harry Stanford.*
Phipps	*Mr. C. H. Brookfield.*
Mason	*Mr. H. Deane.*
James	*Mr. Charles Meyrick.*
Harold	*Mr. Goodhart.*
Lady Chiltern	*Miss Julia Neilson.*
Lady Markby	*Miss Fanny Brough.*
Countess of Basildon	*Miss Vane Featherston.*
Mrs. Marchmont	*Miss Helen Forsyth.*
Miss Mabel Chiltern	*Miss Maud Millet.*
Mrs. Cheveley	*Miss Florence West.*

FIRST ACT

SCENE

The octagon room at Sir Robert Chiltern's house in Grosvenor Square.

[*The room is brilliantly lighted and full of guests. At the top of the staircase stands* lady chiltern, *a woman of grave Greek beauty, about twenty-seven years of age. She receives the guests as they come up. Over the well of the staircase hangs a great chandelier with wax lights, which illumine a large eighteenth-century French tapestry—representing the Triumph of Love, from a design by Boucher— that is stretched on the staircase wall. On the right is the entrance to the music-room. The sound of a string quartette is faintly heard. The entrance on the left leads to other reception-rooms.* mrs. marchmont *and* lady basildon, *two very pretty women, are seated together on a Louis Seize sofa. They are types of exquisite fragility. Their affectation of manner has a delicate charm. Watteau would have loved to paint them.*]

mrs. marchmont. Going on to the Hartlocks' to-night, Margaret?

lady basildon. I suppose so. Are you?

mrs. marchmont. Yes. Horribly tedious parties they give, don't they?

lady basildon. Horribly tedious! Never know why I go. Never know why I go anywhere.

mrs. marchmont. I come here to be educated.

lady basildon. Ah! I hate being educated!

mrs. marchmont. So do I. It puts one almost on a level with the commercial classes, doesn't it? But dear Gertrude Chiltern is always telling me that I should have some serious purpose in life. So I come here to try to find one.

lady basildon. [Looking round through her lorgnette.] I don't see anybody here to-night whom one could possibly call a serious purpose. The man who took me in to dinner talked to me about his wife the whole time.

mrs. marchmont. How very trivial of him!

lady basildon. Terribly trivial! What did your man talk about?

mrs. marchmont. About myself.

lady basildon. [Languidly.] And were you interested?

mrs. marchmont. [Shaking her head.] Not in the smallest degree.

lady basildon. What martyrs we are, dear Margaret!

mrs. marchmont. [Rising.] And how well it becomes us, Olivia!

[*They rise and go towards the music-room.* The vicomte de nanjac, *a young attaché known for his neckties and his Anglomania, approaches with a low bow, and enters into conversation.*]

mason. [Announcing guests from the top of the staircase.] Mr. and Lady Jane Barford. Lord Caversham.

[Enter lord caversham, an old gentleman of seventy, wearing the riband and star of the Garter. A fine Whig type. Rather like a portrait by Lawrence.]

lord caversham. Good evening, Lady Chiltern! Has my good-for-nothing young son been here?

lady chiltern. [Smiling.] I don't think Lord Goring has arrived yet.

mabel chiltern. [Coming up to lord caversham.] Why do you call Lord Goring good-for-nothing?

[mabel chiltern *is a perfect example of the English type of prettiness, the apple-blossom type. She has all the fragrance and freedom of a flower. There is ripple after ripple of sunlight in her hair, and the little mouth, with its parted lips, is expectant, like the mouth of a child. She has the fascinating tyranny of youth, and the astonishing courage of innocence. To sane people she is not reminiscent of any work of art. But she is really like a Tanagra statuette, and would be rather annoyed if she were told so.*]

18

lord caversham. Because he leads such an idle life.

mabel chiltern. How can you say such a thing? Why, he rides in the Row at ten o'clock in the morning, goes to the Opera three times a week, changes his clothes at least five times a day, and dines out every night of the season. You don't call that leading an idle life, do you?

lord caversham. [Looking at her with a kindly twinkle in his eyes.] You are a very charming young lady!

mabel chiltern. How sweet of you to say that, Lord Caversham! Do come to us more often. You know we are always at home on Wednesdays, and you look so well with your star!

lord caversham. Never go anywhere now. Sick of London Society. Shouldn't mind being introduced to my own tailor; he always votes on the right side. But object strongly to being sent down to dinner with my wife's milliner. Never could stand Lady Caversham's bonnets.

mabel chiltern. Oh, I love London Society! I think it has immensely improved. It is entirely composed now of beautiful idiots and brilliant lunatics. Just what Society should be.

lord caversham. Hum! Which is Goring? Beautiful idiot, or the other thing?

mabel chiltern. [Gravely.] I have been obliged for the present to put Lord Goring into a class quite by himself. But he is developing charmingly!

lord caversham. Into what?

mabel chiltern. [With a little curtsey.] I hope to let you know very soon, Lord Caversham!

mason. [Announcing guests.] Lady Markby. Mrs. Cheveley.

[*Enter* lady markby *and* mrs. cheveley. lady markby *is a pleasant, kindly, popular woman, with gray hair à la marquise and good lace.* mrs. cheveley, *who accompanies her, is tall and rather slight. Lips very thin and highly-coloured, a line of scarlet on a pallid face. Venetian red hair, aquiline nose, and long throat.*

Rouge accentuates the natural paleness of her complexion. Gray-green eyes that move restlessly. She is in heliotrope, with diamonds. She looks rather like an orchid, and makes great demands on one's curiosity. In all her movements she is extremely graceful. A work of art, on the whole, but showing the influence of too many schools.]

lady markby. Good evening, dear Gertrude! So kind of you to let me bring my friend, Mrs. Cheveley. Two such charming women should know each other!

lady chiltern. [Advances towards mrs. cheveley with a sweet smile. Then suddenly stops, and bows rather distantly.] I think Mrs. Cheveley and I have met before. I did not know she had married a second time.

lady markby. [Genially.] Ah, nowadays people marry as often as they can, don't they? It is most fashionable. [To duchess of maryborough.] Dear Duchess, and how is the Duke? Brain still weak, I suppose? Well, that is only to be expected, is it not? His good father was just the same. There is nothing like race, is there?

mrs. cheveley. [Playing with her fan.] But have we really met before, Lady Chiltern? I can't remember where. I have been out of England for so long.

lady chiltern. We were at school together, Mrs. Cheveley.

mrs. cheveley [Superciliously.] Indeed? I have forgotten all about my schooldays. I have a vague impression that they were detestable.

lady chiltern. [Coldly.] I am not surprised!

mrs. cheveley. [In her sweetest manner.] Do you know, I am quite looking forward to meeting your clever husband, Lady Chiltern. Since he has been at the Foreign Office, he has been so much talked of in Vienna. They actually succeed in spelling his name right in the newspapers. That in itself is fame, on the continent.

lady chiltern. I hardly think there will be much in common between you and my husband, Mrs. Cheveley! [Moves away.]

20

vicomte de nanjac. Ah! chère Madame, queue surprise! I have not seen you since Berlin!

mrs. cheveley. Not since Berlin, Vicomte. Five years ago!

vicomte de nanjac. And you are younger and more beautiful than ever. How do you manage it?

mrs. cheveley. By making it a rule only to talk to perfectly charming people like yourself.

vicomte de nanjac. Ah! you flatter me. You butter me, as they say here.

mrs. cheveley. Do they say that here? How dreadful of them!

vicomte de nanjac. Yes, they have a wonderful language. It should be more widely known.

[sir robert chiltern *enters. A man of forty, but looking somewhat younger. Clean-shaven, with finely-cut features, dark-haired and dark-eyed. A personality of mark. Not popular—few personalities are. But intensely admired by the few, and deeply respected by the many. The note of his manner is that of perfect distinction, with a slight touch of pride. One feels that he is conscious of the success he has made in life. A nervous temperament, with a tired look. The firmly-chiselled mouth and chin contrast strikingly with the romantic expression in the deep-set eyes. The variance is suggestive of an almost complete separation of passion and intellect, as though thought and emotion were each isolated in its own sphere through some violence of will-power. There is nervousness in the nostrils, and in the pale, thin, pointed hands. It would be inaccurate to call him picturesque. Picturesqueness cannot survive the House of Commons. But Vandyck would have liked to have painted his head.*]

sir robert chiltern. Good evening, Lady Markby! I hope you have brought Sir John with you?

lady markby. Oh! I have brought a much more charming person than Sir John. Sir John's temper since he has taken seriously to politics has become quite unbearable. Really, now that the House of Commons is trying to become useful, it does a great deal of harm.

sir robert chiltern. I hope not, Lady Markby. At any rate we do our best to waste the public time, don't we? But who is this charming person you have been kind enough to bring to us?

lady markby. Her name is Mrs. Cheveley! One of the Dorsetshire Cheveleys, I suppose. But I really don't know. Families are so mixed nowadays. Indeed, as a rule, everybody turns out to be somebody else.

sir robert chiltern. Mrs. Cheveley? I seem to know the name.

lady markby. She has just arrived from Vienna.

sir robert chiltern. Ah! yes. I think I know whom you mean.

lady markby. Oh! she goes everywhere there, and has such pleasant scandals about all her friends. I really must go to Vienna next winter. I hope there is a good chef at the Embassy.

sir robert chiltern. If there is not, the Ambassador will certainly have to be recalled. Pray point out Mrs. Cheveley to me. I should like to see her.

lady markby. Let me introduce you. [To mrs. cheveley.] My dear, Sir Robert Chiltern is dying to know you!

sir robert chiltern. [Bowing.] Every one is dying to know the brilliant Mrs. Cheveley. Our attachés at Vienna write to us about nothing else.

mrs. cheveley. Thank you, Sir Robert. An acquaintance that begins with a compliment is sure to develop into a real friendship. It starts in the right manner. And I find that I know Lady Chiltern already.

sir robert chiltern. Really?

mrs. cheveley. Yes. She has just reminded me that we were at school together. I remember it perfectly now. She always got the good conduct prize. I have a distinct recollection of Lady Chiltern always getting the good conduct prize!

sir robert chiltern. [Smiling.] And what prizes did you get, Mrs. Cheveley?

mrs. cheveley. My prizes came a little later on in life. I don't think any of them were for good conduct. I forget!

sir robert chiltern. I am sure they were for something charming!

mrs. cheveley. I don't know that women are always rewarded for being charming. I think they are usually punished for it! Certainly, more women grow old nowadays through the faithfulness of their admirers than through anything else! At least that is the only way I can account for the terribly haggard look of most of your pretty women in London!

sir robert chiltern. What an appalling philosophy that sounds! To attempt to classify you, Mrs. Cheveley, would be an impertinence. But may I ask, at heart, are you an optimist or a pessimist? Those seem to be the only two fashionable religions left to us nowadays.

mrs. cheveley. Oh, I'm neither. Optimism begins in a broad grin, and Pessimism ends with blue spectacles. Besides, they are both of them merely poses.

sir robert chiltern. You prefer to be natural?

mrs. cheveley. Sometimes. But it is such a very difficult pose to keep up.

sir robert chiltern. What would those modern psychological novelists, of whom we hear so much, say to such a theory as that?

mrs. cheveley. Ah! the strength of women comes from the fact that psychology cannot explain us. Men can be analysed, women . . . merely adored.

sir robert chiltern. You think science cannot grapple with the problem of women?

mrs. cheveley. Science can never grapple with the irrational. That is why it has no future before it, in this world.

sir robert chiltern. And women represent the irrational.

mrs. cheveley. Well-dressed women do.

sir robert chiltern. [With a polite bow.] I fear I could hardly agree with you there. But do sit down. And now tell me, what makes you leave your brilliant Vienna for our gloomy London—or perhaps the question is indiscreet?

mrs. cheveley. Questions are never indiscreet. Answers sometimes are.

sir robert chiltern. Well, at any rate, may I know if it is politics or pleasure?

mrs. cheveley. Politics are my only pleasure. You see nowadays it is not fashionable to flirt till one is forty, or to be romantic till one is forty-five, so we poor women who are under thirty, or say we are, have nothing open to us but politics or philanthropy. And philanthropy seems to me to have become simply the refuge of people who wish to annoy their fellow-creatures. I prefer politics. I think they are more . . . becoming!

sir robert chiltern. A political life is a noble career!

mrs. cheveley. Sometimes. And sometimes it is a clever game, Sir Robert. And sometimes it is a great nuisance.

sir robert chiltern. Which do you find it?

mrs. cheveley. I? A combination of all three. [Drops her fan.]

sir robert chiltern. [Picks up fan.] Allow me!

mrs. cheveley. Thanks.

sir robert chiltern. But you have not told me yet what makes you honour London so suddenly. Our season is almost over.

mrs. cheveley. Oh! I don't care about the London season! It is too matrimonial. People are either hunting for husbands, or hiding from them. I wanted to meet you. It is quite true. You know what a woman's curiosity is. Almost as great as a man's! I wanted immensely to meet you, and . . . to ask you to do something for me.

sir robert chiltern. I hope it is not a little thing, Mrs. Cheveley. I find

24

that little things are so very difficult to do.

mrs. cheveley. [After a moment's reflection.] No, I don't think it is quite a little thing.

sir robert chiltern. I am so glad. Do tell me what it is.

mrs. cheveley. Later on. [Rises.] And now may I walk through your beautiful house? I hear your pictures are charming. Poor Baron Arnheim—you remember the Baron?—used to tell me you had some wonderful Corots.

sir robert chiltern. [With an almost imperceptible start.] Did you know Baron Arnheim well?

mrs. cheveley. [Smiling.] Intimately. Did you?

sir robert chiltern. At one time.

mrs. cheveley. Wonderful man, wasn't he?

sir robert chiltern. [After a pause.] He was very remarkable, in many ways.

mrs. cheveley. I often think it such a pity he never wrote his memoirs. They would have been most interesting.

sir robert chiltern. Yes: he knew men and cities well, like the old Greek.

mrs. cheveley. Without the dreadful disadvantage of having a Penelope waiting at home for him.

mason. Lord Goring.

[Enter lord goring. *Thirty-four, but always says he is younger. A well-bred, expressionless face. He is clever, but would not like to be thought so. A flawless dandy, he would be annoyed if he were considered romantic. He plays with life, and is on perfectly good terms with the world. He is fond of being misunderstood. It gives him a post of vantage.*]

sir robert chiltern. Good evening, my dear Arthur! Mrs. Cheveley, allow me to introduce to you Lord Goring, the idlest man in London.

mrs. cheveley. I have met Lord Goring before.

lord goring. [Bowing.] I did not think you would remember me, Mrs. Cheveley.

mrs. cheveley. My memory is under admirable control. And are you still a bachelor?

lord goring. I . . . believe so.

mrs. cheveley. How very romantic!

lord goring. Oh! I am not at all romantic. I am not old enough. I leave romance to my seniors.

sir robert chiltern. Lord Goring is the result of Boodle's Club, Mrs. Cheveley.

mrs. cheveley. He reflects every credit on the institution.

lord goring. May I ask are you staying in London long?

mrs. cheveley. That depends partly on the weather, partly on the cooking, and partly on Sir Robert.

sir robert chiltern. You are not going to plunge us into a European war, I hope?

mrs. cheveley. There is no danger, at present!

[*She nods to* lord goring, *with a look of amusement in her eyes, and goes out with* sir robert chiltern. lord goring *saunters over to* mabel chiltern.]

mabel chiltern. You are very late!

lord goring. Have you missed me?

mabel chiltern. Awfully!

lord goring. Then I am sorry I did not stay away longer. I like being missed.

mabel chiltern. How very selfish of you!

lord goring. I am very selfish.

mabel chiltern. You are always telling me of your bad qualities, Lord Goring.

lord goring. I have only told you half of them as yet, Miss Mabel!

mabel chiltern. Are the others very bad?

lord goring. Quite dreadful! When I think of them at night I go to sleep at once.

mabel chiltern. Well, I delight in your bad qualities. I wouldn't have you part with one of them.

lord goring. How very nice of you! But then you are always nice. By the way, I want to ask you a question, Miss Mabel. Who brought Mrs. Cheveley here? That woman in heliotrope, who has just gone out of the room with your brother?

mabel chiltern. Oh, I think Lady Markby brought her. Why do you ask?

lord goring. I haven't seen her for years, that is all.

mabel chiltern. What an absurd reason!

lord goring. All reasons are absurd.

mabel chiltern. What sort of a woman is she?

lord goring. Oh! a genius in the daytime and a beauty at night!

mabel chiltern. I dislike her already.

lord goring. That shows your admirable good taste.

vicomte de nanjac. [Approaching.] Ah, the English young lady is the dragon of good taste, is she not? Quite the dragon of good taste.

lord goring. So the newspapers are always telling us.

vicomte de nanjac. I read all your English newspapers. I find them so amusing.

lord goring. Then, my dear Nanjac, you must certainly read between the lines.

vicomte de nanjac. I should like to, but my professor objects. [To mabel chiltern.] May I have the pleasure of escorting you to the music-room, Mademoiselle?

mabel chiltern. [Looking very disappointed.] Delighted, Vicomte, quite delighted! [Turning to lord goring.] Aren't you coming to the music-room?

lord goring. Not if there is any music going on, Miss Mabel.

mabel chiltern. [Severely.] The music is in German. You would not understand it.

[*Goes out with the v*icomte de nanjac. lord caversham *comes up to his son.*]

lord caversham. Well, sir! what are you doing here? Wasting your life as usual! You should be in bed, sir. You keep too late hours! I heard of you the other night at Lady Rufford's dancing till four o'clock in the morning!

lord goring. Only a quarter to four, father.

lord caversham. Can't make out how you stand London Society. The thing has gone to the dogs, a lot of damned nobodies talking about nothing.

lord goring. I love talking about nothing, father. It is the only thing I know anything about.

lord caversham. You seem to me to be living entirely for pleasure.

lord goring. What else is there to live for, father? Nothing ages like happiness.

lord caversham. You are heartless, sir, very heartless!

lord goring. I hope not, father. Good evening, Lady Basildon!

28

lady basildon. [Arching two pretty eyebrows.] Are you here? I had no idea you ever came to political parties!

lord goring. I adore political parties. They are the only place left to us where people don't talk politics.

lady basildon. I delight in talking politics. I talk them all day long. But I can't bear listening to them. I don't know how the unfortunate men in the House stand these long debates.

lord goring. By never listening.

lady basildon. Really?

lord goring. [In his most serious manner.] Of course. You see, it is a very dangerous thing to listen. If one listens one may be convinced; and a man who allows himself to be convinced by an argument is a thoroughly unreasonable person.

lady basildon. Ah! that accounts for so much in men that I have never understood, and so much in women that their husbands never appreciate in them!

mrs. marchmont. [With a sigh.] Our husbands never appreciate anything in us. We have to go to others for that!

lady basildon. [Emphatically.] Yes, always to others, have we not?

lord goring. [Smiling.] And those are the views of the two ladies who are known to have the most admirable husbands in London.

mrs. marchmont. That is exactly what we can't stand. My Reginald is quite hopelessly faultless. He is really unendurably so, at times! There is not the smallest element of excitement in knowing him.

lord goring. How terrible! Really, the thing should be more widely known!

lady basildon. Basildon is quite as bad; he is as domestic as if he was a bachelor.

mrs. marchmont. [Pressing lady basildon's hand.] My poor Olivia! We have married perfect husbands, and we are well punished for it.

lord goring. I should have thought it was the husbands who were punished.

mrs. marchmont. [Drawing herself up.] Oh, dear no! They are as happy as possible! And as for trusting us, it is tragic how much they trust us.

lady basildon. Perfectly tragic!

lord goring. Or comic, Lady Basildon?

lady basildon. Certainly not comic, Lord Goring. How unkind of you to suggest such a thing!

mrs. marchmont. I am afraid Lord Goring is in the camp of the enemy, as usual. I saw him talking to that Mrs. Cheveley when he came in.

lord goring. Handsome woman, Mrs. Cheveley!

lady basildon. [Stiffly.] Please don't praise other women in our presence. You might wait for us to do that!

lord goring. I did wait.

mrs. marchmont. Well, we are not going to praise her. I hear she went to the Opera on Monday night, and told Tommy Rufford at supper that, as far as she could see, London Society was entirely made up of dowdies and dandies.

lord goring. She is quite right, too. The men are all dowdies and the women are all dandies, aren't they?

mrs. marchmont. [After a pause.] Oh! do you really think that is what Mrs. Cheveley meant?

lord goring. Of course. And a very sensible remark for Mrs. Cheveley to make, too.

[*Enter* mabel chiltern. *She joins the group.*]

mabel chiltern. Why are you talking about Mrs. Cheveley? Everybody is talking about Mrs. Cheveley! Lord Goring says—what did you say, Lord Goring, about Mrs. Cheveley? Oh! I remember, that she was a genius in the daytime and a beauty at night.

lady basildon. What a horrid combination! So very unnatural!

mrs. marchmont. [In her most dreamy manner.] I like looking at geniuses, and listening to beautiful people.

lord goring. Ah! that is morbid of you, Mrs. Marchmont!

mrs. marchmont. [Brightening to a look of real pleasure.] I am so glad to hear you say that. Marchmont and I have been married for seven years, and he has never once told me that I was morbid. Men are so painfully unobservant!

lady basildon. [Turning to her.] I have always said, dear Margaret, that you were the most morbid person in London.

mrs. marchmont. Ah! but you are always sympathetic, Olivia!

mabel chiltern. Is it morbid to have a desire for food? I have a great desire for food. Lord Goring, will you give me some supper?

lord goring. With pleasure, Miss Mabel. [Moves away with her.]

mabel chiltern. How horrid you have been! You have never talked to me the whole evening!

lord goring. How could I? You went away with the child-diplomatist.

mabel chiltern. You might have followed us. Pursuit would have been only polite. I don't think I like you at all this evening!

lord goring. I like you immensely.

mabel chiltern. Well, I wish you'd show it in a more marked way! [They go downstairs.]

mrs. marchmont. Olivia, I have a curious feeling of absolute faintness.

I think I should like some supper very much. I know I should like some supper.

lady basildon. I am positively dying for supper, Margaret!

mrs. marchmont. Men are so horribly selfish, they never think of these things.

lady basildon. Men are grossly material, grossly material!

[*The* vicomte de nanjac *enters from the music-room with some other guests. After having carefully examined all the people present, he approaches* lady basildon.]

vicomte de nanjac. May I have the honour of taking you down to supper, Comtesse?

lady basildon. [Coldly.] I never take supper, thank you, Vicomte. [The vicomte is about to retire. lady basildon, seeing this, rises at once and takes his arm.] But I will come down with you with pleasure.

vicomte de nanjac. I am so fond of eating! I am very English in all my tastes.

lady basildon. You look quite English, Vicomte, quite English.

[*They pass out.* mr. montford, *a perfectly groomed young dandy, approaches* mrs. marchmont.]

mr. montford. Like some supper, Mrs. Marchmont?

mrs. marchmont. [Languidly.] Thank you, Mr. Montford, I never touch supper. [Rises hastily and takes his arm.] But I will sit beside you, and watch you.

mr. montford. I don't know that I like being watched when I am eating!

mrs. marchmont. Then I will watch some one else.

mr. montford. I don't know that I should like that either.

mrs. marchmont. [Severely.] Pray, Mr. Montford, do not make these painful scenes of jealousy in public!

[*They go downstairs with the other guests, passing* sir robert chiltern *and* mrs. cheveley, *who now enter.*]

sir robert chiltern. And are you going to any of our country houses before you leave England, Mrs. Cheveley?

mrs. cheveley. Oh, no! I can't stand your English house-parties. In England people actually try to be brilliant at breakfast. That is so dreadful of them! Only dull people are brilliant at breakfast. And then the family skeleton is always reading family prayers. My stay in England really depends on you, Sir Robert. [Sits down on the sofa.]

sir robert chiltern. [Taking a seat beside her.] Seriously?

mrs. cheveley. Quite seriously. I want to talk to you about a great political and financial scheme, about this Argentine Canal Company, in fact.

sir robert chiltern. What a tedious, practical subject for you to talk about, Mrs. Cheveley!

mrs. cheveley. Oh, I like tedious, practical subjects. What I don't like are tedious, practical people. There is a wide difference. Besides, you are interested, I know, in International Canal schemes. You were Lord Radley's secretary, weren't you, when the Government bought the Suez Canal shares?

sir robert chiltern. Yes. But the Suez Canal was a very great and splendid undertaking. It gave us our direct route to India. It had imperial value. It was necessary that we should have control. This Argentine scheme is a commonplace Stock Exchange swindle.

mrs. cheveley. A speculation, Sir Robert! A brilliant, daring speculation.

sir robert chiltern. Believe me, Mrs. Cheveley, it is a swindle. Let us call things by their proper names. It makes matters simpler. We have all the information about it at the Foreign Office. In fact, I sent out a special Commission to inquire into the matter privately, and they report that the works are hardly begun, and as for the money already subscribed, no one seems to know what has become of it. The whole thing is a second Panama, and with not a quarter of the chance of success that miserable affair ever had. I hope you have not invested in it. I am sure you are far too clever to have done that.

mrs. cheveley. I have invested very largely in it.

sir robert chiltern. Who could have advised you to do such a foolish thing?

mrs. cheveley. Your old friend—and mine.

sir robert chiltern. Who?

mrs. cheveley. Baron Arnheim.

sir robert chiltern. [Frowning.] Ah! yes. I remember hearing, at the time of his death, that he had been mixed up in the whole affair.

mrs. cheveley. It was his last romance. His last but one, to do him justice.

sir robert chiltern. [Rising.] But you have not seen my Corots yet. They are in the music-room. Corots seem to go with music, don't they? May I show them to you?

mrs. cheveley. [Shaking her head.] I am not in a mood to-night for silver twilights, or rose-pink dawns. I want to talk business. [Motions to him with her fan to sit down again beside her.]

sir robert chiltern. I fear I have no advice to give you, Mrs. Cheveley, except to interest yourself in something less dangerous. The success of the Canal depends, of course, on the attitude of England, and I am going to lay the report of the Commissioners before the House to-morrow night.

mrs. cheveley. That you must not do. In your own interests, Sir Robert, to say nothing of mine, you must not do that.

sir robert chiltern. [Looking at her in wonder.] In my own interests? My dear Mrs. Cheveley, what do you mean? [Sits down beside her.]

mrs. cheveley. Sir Robert, I will be quite frank with you. I want you to withdraw the report that you had intended to lay before the House, on the ground that you have reasons to believe that the Commissioners have been prejudiced or misinformed, or something. Then I want you to say a few words to the effect that the Government is going to reconsider the question, and that you have reason to believe that the Canal, if completed, will be of great international value. You know the sort of things ministers say in cases of this kind. A few ordinary platitudes will do. In modern life nothing produces such an effect as a good platitude. It makes the whole world kin. Will you do that for me?

sir robert chiltern. Mrs. Cheveley, you cannot be serious in making me such a proposition!

mrs. cheveley. I am quite serious.

sir robert chiltern. [Coldly.] Pray allow me to believe that you are not.

mrs. cheveley. [Speaking with great deliberation and emphasis.] Ah! but I am. And if you do what I ask you, I . . . will pay you very handsomely!

sir robert chiltern. Pay me!

mrs. cheveley. Yes.

sir robert chiltern. I am afraid I don't quite understand what you mean.

mrs. cheveley. [Leaning back on the sofa and looking at him.] How very disappointing! And I have come all the way from Vienna in order that you should thoroughly understand me.

sir robert chiltern. I fear I don't.

mrs. cheveley. [In her most nonchalant manner.] My dear Sir Robert, you are a man of the world, and you have your price, I suppose. Everybody has nowadays. The drawback is that most people are so dreadfully expensive. I know I am. I hope you will be more reasonable in your terms.

sir robert chiltern. [Rises indignantly.] If you will allow me, I will call your carriage for you. You have lived so long abroad, Mrs. Cheveley, that you seem to be unable to realise that you are talking to an English gentleman.

mrs. cheveley. [Detains him by touching his arm with her fan, and keeping it there while she is talking.] I realise that I am talking to a man who laid the foundation of his fortune by selling to a Stock Exchange speculator a Cabinet secret.

sir robert chiltern. [Biting his lip.] What do you mean?

mrs. cheveley. [Rising and facing him.] I mean that I know the real origin of your wealth and your career, and I have got your letter, too.

sir robert chiltern. What letter?

mrs. cheveley. [Contemptuously.] The letter you wrote to Baron Arnheim, when you were Lord Radley's secretary, telling the Baron to buy Suez Canal shares—a letter written three days before the Government announced its own purchase.

sir robert chiltern. [Hoarsely.] It is not true.

mrs. cheveley. You thought that letter had been destroyed. How foolish of you! It is in my possession.

sir robert chiltern. The affair to which you allude was no more than a speculation. The House of Commons had not yet passed the bill; it might have been rejected.

mrs. cheveley. It was a swindle, Sir Robert. Let us call things by their proper names. It makes everything simpler. And now I am going to sell you that letter, and the price I ask for it is your public support of the Argentine scheme. You made your own fortune out of one canal. You must help me and my friends to make our fortunes out of another!

sir robert chiltern. It is infamous, what you propose—infamous!

mrs. cheveley. Oh, no! This is the game of life as we all have to play it, Sir Robert, sooner or later!

sir robert chiltern. I cannot do what you ask me.

mrs. cheveley. You mean you cannot help doing it. You know you are standing on the edge of a precipice. And it is not for you to make terms. It is for you to accept them. Supposing you refuse—

sir robert chiltern. What then?

mrs. cheveley. My dear Sir Robert, what then? You are ruined, that is all! Remember to what a point your Puritanism in England has brought you. In old days nobody pretended to be a bit better than his neighbours. In fact, to be a bit better than one's neighbour was considered excessively vulgar and middle-class. Nowadays, with our modern mania for morality, every one has to pose as a paragon of purity, incorruptibility, and all the other seven deadly virtues—and what is the result? You all go over like ninepins—one after the other. Not a year passes in England without somebody disappearing. Scandals used to lend charm, or at least interest, to a man—now they crush him. And yours is a very nasty scandal. You couldn't survive it. If it were known that as a young man, secretary to a great and important minister, you sold a Cabinet secret for a large sum of money, and that that was the origin of your wealth and career, you would be hounded out of public life, you would disappear completely. And after all, Sir Robert, why should you sacrifice your entire future rather than deal diplomatically with your enemy? For the moment I am your enemy. I admit it! And I am much stronger than you are. The big battalions are on my side. You have a splendid position, but it is your splendid position that makes you so vulnerable. You can't defend it! And I am in attack. Of course I have not talked morality to you. You must admit in fairness that I have spared you that. Years ago you did a clever, unscrupulous thing; it turned out a great success. You owe to it your fortune and position. And now you have got to pay for it. Sooner or later we have all to pay for what we do. You have to pay now. Before I leave you to-night, you have got to promise me to suppress your report, and to speak in the House in favour of this scheme.

sir robert chiltern. What you ask is impossible.

mrs. cheveley. You must make it possible. You are going to make it possible. Sir Robert, you know what your English newspapers are like.

Suppose that when I leave this house I drive down to some newspaper office, and give them this scandal and the proofs of it! Think of their loathsome joy, of the delight they would have in dragging you down, of the mud and mire they would plunge you in. Think of the hypocrite with his greasy smile penning his leading article, and arranging the foulness of the public placard.

sir robert chiltern. Stop! You want me to withdraw the report and to make a short speech stating that I believe there are possibilities in the scheme?

mrs. cheveley. [Sitting down on the sofa.] Those are my terms.

sir robert chiltern. [In a low voice.] I will give you any sum of money you want.

mrs. cheveley. Even you are not rich enough, Sir Robert, to buy back your past. No man is.

sir robert chiltern. I will not do what you ask me. I will not.

mrs. cheveley. You have to. If you don't . . . [Rises from the sofa.]

sir robert chiltern. [Bewildered and unnerved.] Wait a moment! What did you propose? You said that you would give me back my letter, didn't you?

mrs. cheveley. Yes. That is agreed. I will be in the Ladies' Gallery to-morrow night at half-past eleven. If by that time—and you will have had heaps of opportunity—you have made an announcement to the House in the terms I wish, I shall hand you back your letter with the prettiest thanks, and the best, or at any rate the most suitable, compliment I can think of. I intend to play quite fairly with you. One should always play fairly . . . when one has the winning cards. The Baron taught me that . . . amongst other things.

sir robert chiltern. You must let me have time to consider your proposal.

mrs. cheveley. No; you must settle now!

sir robert chiltern. Give me a week—three days!

mrs. cheveley. Impossible! I have got to telegraph to Vienna to-night.

sir robert chiltern. My God! what brought you into my life?

mrs. cheveley. Circumstances. [Moves towards the door.]

sir robert chiltern. Don't go. I consent. The report shall be withdrawn. I will arrange for a question to be put to me on the subject.

mrs. cheveley. Thank you. I knew we should come to an amicable agreement. I understood your nature from the first. I analysed you, though you did not adore me. And now you can get my carriage for me, Sir Robert. I see the people coming up from supper, and Englishmen always get romantic after a meal, and that bores me dreadfully. [Exit sir robert chiltern.]

[*Enter Guests,* lady chiltern, lady markby, lord caversham, lady basildon, mrs. marchmont, vicomte de nanjac, mr. montford.]

lady markby. Well, dear Mrs. Cheveley, I hope you have enjoyed yourself. Sir Robert is very entertaining, is he not?

mrs. cheveley. Most entertaining! I have enjoyed my talk with him immensely.

lady markby. He has had a very interesting and brilliant career. And he has married a most admirable wife. Lady Chiltern is a woman of the very highest principles, I am glad to say. I am a little too old now, myself, to trouble about setting a good example, but I always admire people who do. And Lady Chiltern has a very ennobling effect on life, though her dinner-parties are rather dull sometimes. But one can't have everything, can one? And now I must go, dear. Shall I call for you to-morrow?

mrs. cheveley. Thanks.

lady markby. We might drive in the Park at five. Everything looks so fresh in the Park now!

mrs. cheveley. Except the people!

lady markby. Perhaps the people are a little jaded. I have often observed that the Season as it goes on produces a kind of softening of the brain. However, I think anything is better than high intellectual pressure. That is the most unbecoming thing there is. It makes the noses of the young girls so particularly large. And there is nothing so difficult to marry as a large nose; men don't like them. Good-night, dear! [To lady chiltern.] Good-night, Gertrude! [Goes out on lord caversham's arm.]

mrs. cheveley. What a charming house you have, Lady Chiltern! I have spent a delightful evening. It has been so interesting getting to know your husband.

lady chiltern. Why did you wish to meet my husband, Mrs. Cheveley?

mrs. cheveley. Oh, I will tell you. I wanted to interest him in this Argentine Canal scheme, of which I dare say you have heard. And I found him most susceptible,—susceptible to reason, I mean. A rare thing in a man. I converted him in ten minutes. He is going to make a speech in the House to-morrow night in favour of the idea. We must go to the Ladies' Gallery and hear him! It will be a great occasion!

lady chiltern. There must be some mistake. That scheme could never have my husband's support.

mrs. cheveley. Oh, I assure you it's all settled. I don't regret my tedious journey from Vienna now. It has been a great success. But, of course, for the next twenty-four hours the whole thing is a dead secret.

lady chiltern. [Gently.] A secret? Between whom?

mrs. cheveley. [With a flash of amusement in her eyes.] Between your husband and myself.

sir robert chiltern. [Entering.] Your carriage is here, Mrs. Cheveley!

mrs. cheveley. Thanks! Good evening, Lady Chiltern! Good-night, Lord Goring! I am at Claridge's. Don't you think you might leave a card?

lord goring. If you wish it, Mrs. Cheveley!

mrs. cheveley. Oh, don't be so solemn about it, or I shall be obliged to leave a card on you. In England I suppose that would hardly be considered en règle. Abroad, we are more civilised. Will you see me down, Sir Robert? Now that we have both the same interests at heart we shall be great friends,

I hope!

[*Sails out on* sir robert chiltern's *arm.* lady chiltern *goes to the top of the staircase and looks down at them as they descend. Her expression is troubled. After a little time she is joined by some of the guests, and passes with them into another reception-room.*]

mabel chiltern. What a horrid woman!

lord goring. You should go to bed, Miss Mabel.

mabel chiltern. Lord Goring!

lord goring. My father told me to go to bed an hour ago. I don't see why I shouldn't give you the same advice. I always pass on good advice. It is the only thing to do with it. It is never of any use to oneself.

mabel chiltern. Lord Goring, you are always ordering me out of the room. I think it most courageous of you. Especially as I am not going to bed for hours. [Goes over to the sofa.] You can come and sit down if you like, and talk about anything in the world, except the Royal Academy, Mrs. Cheveley, or novels in Scotch dialect. They are not improving subjects. [Catches sight of something that is lying on the sofa half hidden by the cushion.] What is this? Some one has dropped a diamond brooch! Quite beautiful, isn't it? [Shows it to him.] I wish it was mine, but Gertrude won't let me wear anything but pearls, and I am thoroughly sick of pearls. They make one look so plain, so good and so intellectual. I wonder whom the brooch belongs to.

lord goring. I wonder who dropped it.

mabel chiltern. It is a beautiful brooch.

lord goring. It is a handsome bracelet.

mabel chiltern. It isn't a bracelet. It's a brooch.

lord goring. It can be used as a bracelet. [Takes it from her, and, pulling out a green letter-case, puts the ornament carefully in it, and replaces the whole thing in his breast-pocket with the most perfect sang froid.]

mabel chiltern. What are you doing?

41

lord goring. Miss Mabel, I am going to make a rather strange request to you.

mabel chiltern. [Eagerly.] Oh, pray do! I have been waiting for it all the evening.

lord goring. [Is a little taken aback, but recovers himself.] Don't mention to anybody that I have taken charge of this brooch. Should any one write and claim it, let me know at once.

mabel chiltern. That is a strange request.

lord goring. Well, you see I gave this brooch to somebody once, years ago.

mabel chiltern. You did?

lord goring. Yes.

[lady chiltern *enters alone. The other guests have gone.*]

mabel chiltern. Then I shall certainly bid you good-night. Good-night, Gertrude! [Exit.]

lady chiltern. Good-night, dear! [To lord goring.] You saw whom Lady Markby brought here to-night?

lord goring. Yes. It was an unpleasant surprise. What did she come here for?

lady chiltern. Apparently to try and lure Robert to uphold some fraudulent scheme in which she is interested. The Argentine Canal, in fact.

lord goring. She has mistaken her man, hasn't she?

lady chiltern. She is incapable of understanding an upright nature like my husband's!

lord goring. Yes. I should fancy she came to grief if she tried to get Robert into her toils. It is extraordinary what astounding mistakes clever women make.

42

lady chiltern. I don't call women of that kind clever. I call them stupid!

lord goring. Same thing often. Good-night, Lady Chiltern!

lady chiltern. Good-night!

[*Enter* sir robert chiltern.]

sir robert chiltern. My dear Arthur, you are not going? Do stop a little!

lord goring. Afraid I can't, thanks. I have promised to look in at the Hartlocks'. I believe they have got a mauve Hungarian band that plays mauve Hungarian music. See you soon. Good-bye!

[*Exit*]

sir robert chiltern. How beautiful you look to-night, Gertrude!

lady chiltern. Robert, it is not true, is it? You are not going to lend your support to this Argentine speculation? You couldn't!

sir robert chiltern. [Starting.] Who told you I intended to do so?

lady chiltern. That woman who has just gone out, Mrs. Cheveley, as she calls herself now. She seemed to taunt me with it. Robert, I know this woman. You don't. We were at school together. She was untruthful, dishonest, an evil influence on every one whose trust or friendship she could win. I hated, I despised her. She stole things, she was a thief. She was sent away for being a thief. Why do you let her influence you?

sir robert chiltern. Gertrude, what you tell me may be true, but it happened many years ago. It is best forgotten! Mrs. Cheveley may have changed since then. No one should be entirely judged by their past.

lady chiltern. [Sadly.] One's past is what one is. It is the only way by which people should be judged.

sir robert chiltern. That is a hard saying, Gertrude!

lady chiltern. It is a true saying, Robert. And what did she mean by boasting that she had got you to lend your support, your name, to a thing I have heard you describe as the most dishonest and fraudulent scheme there has ever been in political life?

sir robert chiltern. [Biting his lip.] I was mistaken in the view I took. We all may make mistakes.

lady chiltern. But you told me yesterday that you had received the report from the Commission, and that it entirely condemned the whole thing.

sir robert chiltern. [Walking up and down.] I have reasons now to believe that the Commission was prejudiced, or, at any rate, misinformed. Besides, Gertrude, public and private life are different things. They have different laws, and move on different lines.

lady chiltern. They should both represent man at his highest. I see no difference between them.

sir robert chiltern. [Stopping.] In the present case, on a matter of practical politics, I have changed my mind. That is all.

lady chiltern. All!

sir robert chiltern. [Sternly.] Yes!

lady chiltern. Robert! Oh! it is horrible that I should have to ask you such a question—Robert, are you telling me the whole truth?

sir robert chiltern. Why do you ask me such a question?

lady chiltern. [After a pause.] Why do you not answer it?

sir robert chiltern. [Sitting down.] Gertrude, truth is a very complex thing, and politics is a very complex business. There are wheels within wheels. One may be under certain obligations to people that one must pay. Sooner or later in political life one has to compromise. Every one does.

lady chiltern. Compromise? Robert, why do you talk so differently to-night from the way I have always heard you talk? Why are you changed?

sir robert chiltern. I am not changed. But circumstances alter things.

lady chiltern. Circumstances should never alter principles!

44

sir robert chiltern. But if I told you—

lady chiltern. What?

sir robert chiltern. That it was necessary, vitally necessary?

lady chiltern. It can never be necessary to do what is not honourable. Or if it be necessary, then what is it that I have loved! But it is not, Robert; tell me it is not. Why should it be? What gain would you get? Money? We have no need of that! And money that comes from a tainted source is a degradation. Power? But power is nothing in itself. It is power to do good that is fine—that, and that only. What is it, then? Robert, tell me why you are going to do this dishonourable thing!

sir robert chiltern. Gertrude, you have no right to use that word. I told you it was a question of rational compromise. It is no more than that.

lady chiltern. Robert, that is all very well for other men, for men who treat life simply as a sordid speculation; but not for you, Robert, not for you. You are different. All your life you have stood apart from others. You have never let the world soil you. To the world, as to myself, you have been an ideal always. Oh! be that ideal still. That great inheritance throw not away— that tower of ivory do not destroy. Robert, men can love what is beneath them—things unworthy, stained, dishonoured. We women worship when we love; and when we lose our worship, we lose everything. Oh! don't kill my love for you, don't kill that!

sir robert chiltern. Gertrude!

lady chiltern. I know that there are men with horrible secrets in their lives—men who have done some shameful thing, and who in some critical moment have to pay for it, by doing some other act of shame—oh! don't tell me you are such as they are! Robert, is there in your life any secret dishonour or disgrace? Tell me, tell me at once, that—

sir robert chiltern. That what?

lady chiltern. [Speaking very slowly.] That our lives may drift apart.

sir robert chiltern. Drift apart?

lady chiltern. That they may be entirely separate. It would be better for us both.

sir robert chiltern. Gertrude, there is nothing in my past life that you might not know.

lady chiltern. I was sure of it, Robert, I was sure of it. But why did you say those dreadful things, things so unlike your real self? Don't let us ever talk about the subject again. You will write, won't you, to Mrs. Cheveley, and tell her that you cannot support this scandalous scheme of hers? If you have given her any promise you must take it back, that is all!

sir robert chiltern. Must I write and tell her that?

lady chiltern. Surely, Robert! What else is there to do?

sir robert chiltern. I might see her personally. It would be better.

lady chiltern. You must never see her again, Robert. She is not a woman you should ever speak to. She is not worthy to talk to a man like you. No; you must write to her at once, now, this moment, and let your letter show her that your decision is quite irrevocable!

sir robert chiltern. Write this moment!

lady chiltern. Yes.

sir robert chiltern. But it is so late. It is close on twelve.

lady chiltern. That makes no matter. She must know at once that she has been mistaken in you—and that you are not a man to do anything base or underhand or dishonourable. Write here, Robert. Write that you decline to support this scheme of hers, as you hold it to be a dishonest scheme. Yes—write the word dishonest. She knows what that word means. [sir robert chiltern sits down and writes a letter. His wife takes it up and reads it.] Yes; that will do. [Rings bell.] And now the envelope. [He writes the envelope slowly. Enter mason.] Have this letter sent at once to Claridge's Hotel. There is no answer. [Exit mason. lady chiltern kneels down beside her husband, and puts her arms around him.] Robert, love gives one an instinct to things.

46

I feel to-night that I have saved you from something that might have been a danger to you, from something that might have made men honour you less than they do. I don't think you realise sufficiently, Robert, that you have brought into the political life of our time a nobler atmosphere, a finer attitude towards life, a freer air of purer aims and higher ideals—I know it, and for that I love you, Robert.

sir robert chiltern. Oh, love me always, Gertrude, love me always!

lady chiltern. I will love you always, because you will always be worthy of love. We needs must love the highest when we see it! [Kisses him and rises and goes out.]

[sir robert chiltern *walks up and down for a moment; then sits down and buries his face in his hands. The Servant enters and begins pulling out the lights.* sir robert chiltern *looks up.*]

sir robert chiltern. Put out the lights, Mason, put out the lights!

[*The Servant puts out the lights. The room becomes almost dark. The only light there is comes from the great chandelier that hangs over the staircase and illumines the tapestry of the Triumph of Love.*]

Act Drop

SECOND ACT

SCENE

Morning-room at Sir Robert Chiltern's house.

[lord goring, *dressed in the height of fashion, is lounging in an armchair.* sir robert chiltern *is standing in front of the fireplace. He is evidently in a state of great mental excitement and distress. As the scene progresses he paces nervously up and down the room.*]

lord goring. My dear Robert, it's a very awkward business, very awkward indeed. You should have told your wife the whole thing. Secrets from other people's wives are a necessary luxury in modern life. So, at least, I am always told at the club by people who are bald enough to know better. But no man should have a secret from his own wife. She invariably finds it out. Women have a wonderful instinct about things. They can discover everything except the obvious.

sir robert chiltern. Arthur, I couldn't tell my wife. When could I have told her? Not last night. It would have made a life-long separation between us, and I would have lost the love of the one woman in the world I worship, of the only woman who has ever stirred love within me. Last night it would have been quite impossible. She would have turned from me in horror . . . in horror and in contempt.

lord goring. Is Lady Chiltern as perfect as all that?

sir robert chiltern. Yes; my wife is as perfect as all that.

lord goring. [Taking off his left-hand glove.] What a pity! I beg your pardon, my dear fellow, I didn't quite mean that. But if what you tell me is true, I should like to have a serious talk about life with Lady Chiltern.

sir robert chiltern. It would be quite useless.

lord goring. May I try?

sir robert chiltern. Yes; but nothing could make her alter her views.

lord goring. Well, at the worst it would simply be a psychological experiment.

sir robert chiltern. All such experiments are terribly dangerous.

lord goring. Everything is dangerous, my dear fellow. If it wasn't so, life wouldn't be worth living. . . . Well, I am bound to say that I think you should have told her years ago.

sir robert chiltern. When? When we were engaged? Do you think she would have married me if she had known that the origin of my fortune is such as it is, the basis of my career such as it is, and that I had done a thing that I suppose most men would call shameful and dishonourable?

lord goring. [Slowly.] Yes; most men would call it ugly names. There is no doubt of that.

sir robert chiltern. [Bitterly.] Men who every day do something of the same kind themselves. Men who, each one of them, have worse secrets in their own lives.

lord goring. That is the reason they are so pleased to find out other people's secrets. It distracts public attention from their own.

sir robert chiltern. And, after all, whom did I wrong by what I did? No one.

lord goring. [Looking at him steadily.] Except yourself, Robert.

sir robert chiltern. [After a pause.] Of course I had private information about a certain transaction contemplated by the Government of the day, and I acted on it. Private information is practically the source of every large modern fortune.

lord goring. [Tapping his boot with his cane.] And public scandal invariably the result.

sir robert chiltern. [Pacing up and down the room.] Arthur, do you think that what I did nearly eighteen years ago should be brought up against me now? Do you think it fair that a man's whole career should be ruined for a fault done in one's boyhood almost? I was twenty-two at the time, and I had the double misfortune of being well-born and poor, two unforgiveable things nowadays. Is it fair that the folly, the sin of one's youth, if men choose to call it a sin, should wreck a life like mine, should place me in the pillory, should shatter all that I have worked for, all that I have built up. Is it fair, Arthur?

lord goring. Life is never fair, Robert. And perhaps it is a good thing for most of us that it is not.

sir robert chiltern. Every man of ambition has to fight his century with its own weapons. What this century worships is wealth. The God of this century is wealth. To succeed one must have wealth. At all costs one must have wealth.

lord goring. You underrate yourself, Robert. Believe me, without wealth you could have succeeded just as well.

sir robert chiltern. When I was old, perhaps. When I had lost my passion for power, or could not use it. When I was tired, worn out, disappointed. I wanted my success when I was young. Youth is the time for success. I couldn't wait.

lord goring. Well, you certainly have had your success while you are still young. No one in our day has had such a brilliant success. Under-Secretary for Foreign Affairs at the age of forty—that's good enough for any one, I should think.

sir robert chiltern. And if it is all taken away from me now? If I lose everything over a horrible scandal? If I am hounded from public life?

lord goring. Robert, how could you have sold yourself for money?

sir robert chiltern. [Excitedly.] I did not sell myself for money. I bought success at a great price. That is all.

lord goring. [Gravely.] Yes; you certainly paid a great price for it. But what first made you think of doing such a thing?

sir robert chiltern. Baron Arnheim.

lord goring. Damned scoundrel!

sir robert chiltern. No; he was a man of a most subtle and refined intellect. A man of culture, charm, and distinction. One of the most intellectual men I ever met.

lord goring. Ah! I prefer a gentlemanly fool any day. There is more to be said for stupidity than people imagine. Personally I have a great admiration for stupidity. It is a sort of fellow-feeling, I suppose. But how did he do it? Tell me the whole thing.

sir robert chiltern. [Throws himself into an armchair by the writing-table.] One night after dinner at Lord Radley's the Baron began talking about success in modern life as something that one could reduce to an absolutely definite science. With that wonderfully fascinating quiet voice of his he expounded to us the most terrible of all philosophies, the philosophy of power, preached to us the most marvellous of all gospels, the gospel of gold. I think he saw the effect he had produced on me, for some days afterwards he wrote and asked me to come and see him. He was living then in Park Lane, in the house Lord Woolcomb has now. I remember so well how, with a strange smile on his pale, curved lips, he led me through his wonderful picture gallery, showed me his tapestries, his enamels, his jewels, his carved ivories, made me wonder at the strange loveliness of the luxury in which he lived; and then told me that luxury was nothing but a background, a painted scene in a play, and that power, power over other men, power over the world, was the one thing worth having, the one supreme pleasure worth knowing, the one joy one never tired of, and that in our century only the rich possessed it.

lord goring. [With great deliberation.] A thoroughly shallow creed.

sir robert chiltern. [Rising.] I didn't think so then. I don't think so now. Wealth has given me enormous power. It gave me at the very outset of my life freedom, and freedom is everything. You have never been poor, and never known what ambition is. You cannot understand what a wonderful chance the Baron gave me. Such a chance as few men get.

lord goring. Fortunately for them, if one is to judge by results. But tell me definitely, how did the Baron finally persuade you to—well, to do what you did?

sir robert chiltern. When I was going away he said to me that if I ever could give him any private information of real value he would make me a very rich man. I was dazed at the prospect he held out to me, and my ambition and my desire for power were at that time boundless. Six weeks later certain private documents passed through my hands.

lord goring. [Keeping his eyes steadily fixed on the carpet.] State documents?

sir robert chiltern. Yes. [lord goring sighs, then passes his hand across his forehead and looks up.]

lord goring. I had no idea that you, of all men in the world, could have been so weak, Robert, as to yield to such a temptation as Baron Arnheim held out to you.

sir robert chiltern. Weak? Oh, I am sick of hearing that phrase. Sick of using it about others. Weak? Do you really think, Arthur, that it is weakness that yields to temptation? I tell you that there are terrible temptations that it requires strength, strength and courage, to yield to. To stake all one's life on a single moment, to risk everything on one throw, whether the stake be power or pleasure, I care not—there is no weakness in that. There is a horrible, a terrible courage. I had that courage. I sat down the same afternoon and wrote Baron Arnheim the letter this woman now holds. He made three-quarters of a million over the transaction.

lord goring. And you?

sir robert chiltern. I received from the Baron £110,000.

lord goring. You were worth more, Robert.

sir robert chiltern. No; that money gave me exactly what I wanted, power over others. I went into the House immediately. The Baron advised me in finance from time to time. Before five years I had almost trebled my fortune. Since then everything that I have touched has turned out a success. In all things connected with money I have had a luck so extraordinary that sometimes it has made me almost afraid. I remember having read somewhere, in some strange book, that when the gods wish to punish us they answer our prayers.

lord goring. But tell me, Robert, did you never suffer any regret for what you had done?

sir robert chiltern. No. I felt that I had fought the century with its own weapons, and won.

lord goring. [Sadly.] You thought you had won.

sir robert chiltern. I thought so. [After a long pause.] Arthur, do you despise me for what I have told you?

lord goring. [With deep feeling in his voice.] I am very sorry for you, Robert, very sorry indeed.

sir robert chiltern. I don't say that I suffered any remorse. I didn't. Not remorse in the ordinary, rather silly sense of the word. But I have paid conscience money many times. I had a wild hope that I might disarm destiny. The sum Baron Arnheim gave me I have distributed twice over in public charities since then.

lord goring. [Looking up.] In public charities? Dear me! what a lot of harm you must have done, Robert!

sir robert chiltern. Oh, don't say that, Arthur; don't talk like that!

lord goring. Never mind what I say, Robert! I am always saying what I shouldn't say. In fact, I usually say what I really think. A great mistake nowadays. It makes one so liable to be misunderstood. As regards this dreadful business, I will help you in whatever way I can. Of course you know that.

sir robert chiltern. Thank you, Arthur, thank you. But what is to be done? What can be done?

lord goring. [Leaning back with his hands in his pockets.] Well, the English can't stand a man who is always saying he is in the right, but they are very fond of a man who admits that he has been in the wrong. It is one of the best things in them. However, in your case, Robert, a confession would not do. The money, if you will allow me to say so, is . . . awkward. Besides, if you did make a clean breast of the whole affair, you would never be able to talk morality again. And in England a man who can't talk morality twice a week to a large, popular, immoral audience is quite over as a serious politician. There would be nothing left for him as a profession except Botany or the Church. A confession would be of no use. It would ruin you.

sir robert chiltern. It would ruin me. Arthur, the only thing for me to do now is to fight the thing out.

lord goring. [Rising from his chair.] I was waiting for you to say that, Robert. It is the only thing to do now. And you must begin by telling your wife the whole story.

sir robert chiltern. That I will not do.

lord goring. Robert, believe me, you are wrong.

sir robert chiltern. I couldn't do it. It would kill her love for me. And now about this woman, this Mrs. Cheveley. How can I defend myself against her? You knew her before, Arthur, apparently.

lord goring. Yes.

sir robert chiltern. Did you know her well?

lord goring. [Arranging his necktie.] So little that I got engaged to be married to her once, when I was staying at the Tenbys'. The affair lasted for three days . . . nearly.

sir robert chiltern. Why was it broken off?

lord goring. [Airily.] Oh, I forget. At least, it makes no matter. By the way, have you tried her with money? She used to be confoundedly fond of money.

sir robert chiltern. I offered her any sum she wanted. She refused.

lord goring. Then the marvellous gospel of gold breaks down sometimes. The rich can't do everything, after all.

sir robert chiltern. Not everything. I suppose you are right. Arthur, I feel that public disgrace is in store for me. I feel certain of it. I never knew what terror was before. I know it now. It is as if a hand of ice were laid upon one's heart. It is as if one's heart were beating itself to death in some empty hollow.

lord goring. [Striking the table.] Robert, you must fight her. You must fight her.

sir robert chiltern. But how?

lord goring. I can't tell you how at present. I have not the smallest idea. But every one has some weak point. There is some flaw in each one of us. [Strolls to the fireplace and looks at himself in the glass.] My father tells me that even I have faults. Perhaps I have. I don't know.

sir robert chiltern. In defending myself against Mrs. Cheveley, I have a right to use any weapon I can find, have I not?

lord goring. [Still looking in the glass.] In your place I don't think I should have the smallest scruple in doing so. She is thoroughly well able to take care of herself.

sir robert chiltern. [Sits down at the table and takes a pen in his hand.] Well, I shall send a cipher telegram to the Embassy at Vienna, to inquire if there is anything known against her. There may be some secret scandal she might be afraid of.

lord goring. [Settling his buttonhole.] Oh, I should fancy Mrs. Cheveley is one of those very modern women of our time who find a new scandal as becoming as a new bonnet, and air them both in the Park every afternoon at five-thirty. I am sure she adores scandals, and that the sorrow of her life at present is that she can't manage to have enough of them.

sir robert chiltern. [Writing.] Why do you say that?

lord goring. [Turning round.] Well, she wore far too much rouge last night, and not quite enough clothes. That is always a sign of despair in a woman.

sir robert chiltern. [Striking a bell.] But it is worth while my wiring to Vienna, is it not?

lord goring. It is always worth while asking a question, though it is not always worth while answering one.

[*Enter* mason.]

sir robert chiltern. Is Mr. Trafford in his room?

mason. Yes, Sir Robert.

sir robert chiltern. [Puts what he has written into an envelope, which he then carefully closes.] Tell him to have this sent off in cipher at once. There must not be a moment's delay.

mason. Yes, Sir Robert.

sir robert chiltern. Oh! just give that back to me again.

[*Writes something on the envelope.* mason *then goes out with the letter.*]

sir robert chiltern. She must have had some curious hold over Baron Arnheim. I wonder what it was.

lord goring. [Smiling.] I wonder.

sir robert chiltern. I will fight her to the death, as long as my wife knows nothing.

lord goring. [Strongly.] Oh, fight in any case—in any case.

sir robert chiltern. [With a gesture of despair.] If my wife found out, there would be little left to fight for. Well, as soon as I hear from Vienna, I shall let you know the result. It is a chance, just a chance, but I believe in it. And as I fought the age with its own weapons, I will fight her with her weapons. It is only fair, and she looks like a woman with a past, doesn't she?

lord goring. Most pretty women do. But there is a fashion in pasts just as there is a fashion in frocks. Perhaps Mrs. Cheveley's past is merely a slightly décolleté one, and they are excessively popular nowadays. Besides, my dear Robert, I should not build too high hopes on frightening Mrs. Cheveley. I should not fancy Mrs. Cheveley is a woman who would be easily frightened. She has survived all her creditors, and she shows wonderful presence of mind.

sir robert chiltern. Oh! I live on hopes now. I clutch at every chance. I feel like a man on a ship that is sinking. The water is round my feet, and the very air is bitter with storm. Hush! I hear my wife's voice.

[*Enter* lady chiltern *in walking dress.*]

lady chiltern. Good afternoon, Lord Goring!

lord goring. Good afternoon, Lady Chiltern! Have you been in the Park?

lady chiltern. No; I have just come from the Woman's Liberal Association, where, by the way, Robert, your name was received with loud applause, and now I have come in to have my tea. [To lord goring.] You will wait and have some tea, won't you?

lord goring. I'll wait for a short time, thanks.

lady chiltern. I will be back in a moment. I am only going to take my hat off.

lord goring. [In his most earnest manner.] Oh! please don't. It is so pretty. One of the prettiest hats I ever saw. I hope the Woman's Liberal Association received it with loud applause.

lady chiltern. [With a smile.] We have much more important work to do than look at each other's bonnets, Lord Goring.

lord goring. Really? What sort of work?

lady chiltern. Oh! dull, useful, delightful things, Factory Acts, Female Inspectors, the Eight Hours' Bill, the Parliamentary Franchise. . . . Everything, in fact, that you would find thoroughly uninteresting.

lord goring. And never bonnets?

lady chiltern. [With mock indignation.] Never bonnets, never!

[lady chiltern goes out through the door leading to her boudoir.]

sir robert chiltern. [Takes lord goring's hand.] You have been a good friend to me, Arthur, a thoroughly good friend.

lord goring. I don't know that I have been able to do much for you, Robert, as yet. In fact, I have not been able to do anything for you, as far as I can see. I am thoroughly disappointed with myself.

sir robert chiltern. You have enabled me to tell you the truth. That is something. The truth has always stifled me.

lord goring. Ah! the truth is a thing I get rid of as soon as possible! Bad habit, by the way. Makes one very unpopular at the club . . . with the older members. They call it being conceited. Perhaps it is.

sir robert chiltern. I would to God that I had been able to tell the truth . . . to live the truth. Ah! that is the great thing in life, to live the truth. [Sighs, and goes towards the door.] I'll see you soon again, Arthur, shan't I?

lord goring. Certainly. Whenever you like. I'm going to look in at the Bachelors' Ball to-night, unless I find something better to do. But I'll come round to-morrow morning. If you should want me to-night by any chance, send round a note to Curzon Street.

sir robert chiltern. Thank you.

[*As he reaches the door,* lady chiltern *enters from her boudoir.*]

lady chiltern. You are not going, Robert?

sir robert chiltern. I have some letters to write, dear.

lady chiltern. [Going to him.] You work too hard, Robert. You seem never to think of yourself, and you are looking so tired.

sir robert chiltern. It is nothing, dear, nothing.

58

[*He kisses her and goes out.*]

lady chiltern. [To lord goring.] Do sit down. I am so glad you have called. I want to talk to you about . . . well, not about bonnets, or the Woman's Liberal Association. You take far too much interest in the first subject, and not nearly enough in the second.

lord goring. You want to talk to me about Mrs. Cheveley?

lady chiltern. Yes. You have guessed it. After you left last night I found out that what she had said was really true. Of course I made Robert write her a letter at once, withdrawing his promise.

lord goring. So he gave me to understand.

lady chiltern. To have kept it would have been the first stain on a career that has been stainless always. Robert must be above reproach. He is not like other men. He cannot afford to do what other men do. [She looks at lord goring, who remains silent.] Don't you agree with me? You are Robert's greatest friend. You are our greatest friend, Lord Goring. No one, except myself, knows Robert better than you do. He has no secrets from me, and I don't think he has any from you.

lord goring. He certainly has no secrets from me. At least I don't think so.

lady chiltern. Then am I not right in my estimate of him? I know I am right. But speak to me frankly.

lord goring. [Looking straight at her.] Quite frankly?

lady chiltern. Surely. You have nothing to conceal, have you?

lord goring. Nothing. But, my dear Lady Chiltern, I think, if you will allow me to say so, that in practical life—

lady chiltern. [Smiling.] Of which you know so little, Lord Goring—

lord goring. Of which I know nothing by experience, though I know something by observation. I think that in practical life there is something about success, actual success, that is a little unscrupulous, something about ambition that is unscrupulous always. Once a man has set his heart and soul on getting to a certain point, if he has to climb the crag, he climbs the crag; if he has to walk in the mire—

lady chiltern. Well?

lord goring. He walks in the mire. Of course I am only talking generally about life.

lady chiltern. [Gravely.] I hope so. Why do you look at me so strangely, Lord Goring?

lord goring. Lady Chiltern, I have sometimes thought that . . . perhaps you are a little hard in some of your views on life. I think that . . . often you don't make sufficient allowances. In every nature there are elements of weakness, or worse than weakness. Supposing, for instance, that—that any public man, my father, or Lord Merton, or Robert, say, had, years ago, written some foolish letter to some one . . .

lady chiltern. What do you mean by a foolish letter?

lord goring. A letter gravely compromising one's position. I am only putting an imaginary case.

lady chiltern. Robert is as incapable of doing a foolish thing as he is of doing a wrong thing.

lord goring. [After a long pause.] Nobody is incapable of doing a foolish thing. Nobody is incapable of doing a wrong thing.

lady chiltern. Are you a Pessimist? What will the other dandies say? They will all have to go into mourning.

lord goring. [Rising.] No, Lady Chiltern, I am not a Pessimist. Indeed I am not sure that I quite know what Pessimism really means. All I do know is that life cannot be understood without much charity, cannot be lived without much charity. It is love, and not German philosophy, that is the true explanation of this world, whatever may be the explanation of the next. And

60

if you are ever in trouble, Lady Chiltern, trust me absolutely, and I will help you in every way I can. If you ever want me, come to me for my assistance, and you shall have it. Come at once to me.

lady chiltern. [Looking at him in surprise.] Lord Goring, you are talking quite seriously. I don't think I ever heard you talk seriously before.

lord goring. [Laughing.] You must excuse me, Lady Chiltern. It won't occur again, if I can help it.

lady chiltern. But I like you to be serious.

[*Enter* mabel chiltern, *in the most ravishing frock.*]

mabel chiltern. Dear Gertrude, don't say such a dreadful thing to Lord Goring. Seriousness would be very unbecoming to him. Good afternoon Lord Goring! Pray be as trivial as you can.

lord goring. I should like to, Miss Mabel, but I am afraid I am . . . a little out of practice this morning; and besides, I have to be going now.

mabel chiltern. Just when I have come in! What dreadful manners you have! I am sure you were very badly brought up.

lord goring. I was.

mabel chiltern. I wish I had brought you up!

lord goring. I am so sorry you didn't.

mabel chiltern. It is too late now, I suppose?

lord goring. [Smiling.] I am not so sure.

mabel chiltern. Will you ride to-morrow morning?

lord goring. Yes, at ten.

mabel chiltern. Don't forget.

lord goring. Of course I shan't. By the way, Lady Chiltern, there is no list of your guests in The Morning Post of to-day. It has apparently

61

been crowded out by the County Council, or the Lambeth Conference, or something equally boring. Could you let me have a list? I have a particular reason for asking you.

lady chiltern. I am sure Mr. Trafford will be able to give you one.

lord goring. Thanks, so much.

mabel chiltern. Tommy is the most useful person in London.

lord goring [Turning to her.] And who is the most ornamental?

mabel chiltern [Triumphantly.] I am.

lord goring. How clever of you to guess it! [Takes up his hat and cane.] Good-bye, Lady Chiltern! You will remember what I said to you, won't you?

lady chiltern. Yes; but I don't know why you said it to me.

lord goring. I hardly know myself. Good-bye, Miss Mabel!

mabel chiltern [With a little moue of disappointment.] I wish you were not going. I have had four wonderful adventures this morning; four and a half, in fact. You might stop and listen to some of them.

lord goring. How very selfish of you to have four and a half! There won't be any left for me.

mabel chiltern. I don't want you to have any. They would not be good for you.

lord goring. That is the first unkind thing you have ever said to me. How charmingly you said it! Ten to-morrow.

mabel chiltern. Sharp.

lord goring. Quite sharp. But don't bring Mr. Trafford.

mabel chiltern. [With a little toss of the head.] Of course I shan't bring Tommy Trafford. Tommy Trafford is in great disgrace.

lord goring. I am delighted to hear it. [Bows and goes out.]

mabel chiltern. Gertrude, I wish you would speak to Tommy Trafford.

lady chiltern. What has poor Mr. Trafford done this time? Robert says he is the best secretary he has ever had.

mabel chiltern. Well, Tommy has proposed to me again. Tommy really does nothing but propose to me. He proposed to me last night in the music-room, when I was quite unprotected, as there was an elaborate trio going on. I didn't dare to make the smallest repartee, I need hardly tell you. If I had, it would have stopped the music at once. Musical people are so absurdly unreasonable. They always want one to be perfectly dumb at the very moment when one is longing to be absolutely deaf. Then he proposed to me in broad daylight this morning, in front of that dreadful statue of Achilles. Really, the things that go on in front of that work of art are quite appalling. The police should interfere. At luncheon I saw by the glare in his eye that he was going to propose again, and I just managed to check him in time by assuring him that I was a bimetallist. Fortunately I don't know what bimetallism means. And I don't believe anybody else does either. But the observation crushed Tommy for ten minutes. He looked quite shocked. And then Tommy is so annoying in the way he proposes. If he proposed at the top of his voice, I should not mind so much. That might produce some effect on the public. But he does it in a horrid confidential way. When Tommy wants to be romantic he talks to one just like a doctor. I am very fond of Tommy, but his methods of proposing are quite out of date. I wish, Gertrude, you would speak to him, and tell him that once a week is quite often enough to propose to any one, and that it should always be done in a manner that attracts some attention.

lady chiltern. Dear Mabel, don't talk like that. Besides, Robert thinks very highly of Mr. Trafford. He believes he has a brilliant future before him.

mabel chiltern. Oh! I wouldn't marry a man with a future before him for anything under the sun.

lady chiltern. Mabel!

mabel chiltern. I know, dear. You married a man with a future, didn't you? But then Robert was a genius, and you have a noble, self-sacrificing character. You can stand geniuses. I have no character at all, and Robert is the only genius I could ever bear. As a rule, I think they are quite impossible. Geniuses talk so much, don't they? Such a bad habit! And they are always thinking about themselves, when I want them to be thinking about me. I must go round now and rehearse at Lady Basildon's. You remember, we are having tableaux, don't you? The Triumph of something, I don't know what! I hope it will be triumph of me. Only triumph I am really interested in at present. [Kisses lady chiltern and goes out; then comes running back.] Oh, Gertrude, do you know who is coming to see you? That dreadful Mrs. Cheveley, in a most lovely gown. Did you ask her?

lady chiltern. [Rising.] Mrs. Cheveley! Coming to see me? Impossible!

mabel chiltern. I assure you she is coming upstairs, as large as life and not nearly so natural.

lady chiltern. You need not wait, Mabel. Remember, Lady Basildon is expecting you.

mabel chiltern. Oh! I must shake hands with Lady Markby. She is delightful. I love being scolded by her.

[*Enter* mason.]

mason. Lady Markby. Mrs. Cheveley.

[*Enter* lady markby *and* mrs. cheveley.]

lady chiltern. [Advancing to meet them.] Dear Lady Markby, how nice of you to come and see me! [Shakes hands with her, and bows somewhat distantly to mrs. cheveley.] Won't you sit down, Mrs. Cheveley?

mrs. cheveley. Thanks. Isn't that Miss Chiltern? I should like so much to know her.

lady chiltern. Mabel, Mrs. Cheveley wishes to know you.

[mabel chiltern *gives a little nod.*]

mrs. cheveley [Sitting down.] I thought your frock so charming last

64

night, Miss Chiltern. So simple and . . . suitable.

mabel chiltern. Really? I must tell my dressmaker. It will be such a surprise to her. Good-bye, Lady Markby!

lady markby. Going already?

mabel chiltern. I am so sorry but I am obliged to. I am just off to rehearsal. I have got to stand on my head in some tableaux.

lady markby. On your head, child? Oh! I hope not. I believe it is most unhealthy. [Takes a seat on the sofa next lady chiltern.]

mabel chiltern. But it is for an excellent charity: in aid of the Undeserving, the only people I am really interested in. I am the secretary, and Tommy Trafford is treasurer.

mrs. cheveley. And what is Lord Goring?

mabel chiltern. Oh! Lord Goring is president.

mrs. cheveley. The post should suit him admirably, unless he has deteriorated since I knew him first.

lady markby. [Reflecting.] You are remarkably modern, Mabel. A little too modern, perhaps. Nothing is so dangerous as being too modern. One is apt to grow old-fashioned quite suddenly. I have known many instances of it.

mabel chiltern. What a dreadful prospect!

lady markby. Ah! my dear, you need not be nervous. You will always be as pretty as possible. That is the best fashion there is, and the only fashion that England succeeds in setting.

mabel chiltern. [With a curtsey.] Thank you so much, Lady Markby, for England . . . and myself. [Goes out.]

lady markby. [Turning to lady chiltern.] Dear Gertrude, we just called to know if Mrs. Cheveley's diamond brooch has been found.

lady chiltern. Here?

mrs. cheveley. Yes. I missed it when I got back to Claridge's, and I thought I might possibly have dropped it here.

lady chiltern. I have heard nothing about it. But I will send for the butler and ask. [Touches the bell.]

mrs. cheveley. Oh, pray don't trouble, Lady Chiltern. I dare say I lost it at the Opera, before we came on here.

lady markby. Ah yes, I suppose it must have been at the Opera. The fact is, we all scramble and jostle so much nowadays that I wonder we have anything at all left on us at the end of an evening. I know myself that, when I am coming back from the Drawing Room, I always feel as if I hadn't a shred on me, except a small shred of decent reputation, just enough to prevent the lower classes making painful observations through the windows of the carriage. The fact is that our Society is terribly over-populated. Really, some one should arrange a proper scheme of assisted emigration. It would do a great deal of good.

mrs. cheveley. I quite agree with you, Lady Markby. It is nearly six years since I have been in London for the Season, and I must say Society has become dreadfully mixed. One sees the oddest people everywhere.

lady markby. That is quite true, dear. But one needn't know them. I'm sure I don't know half the people who come to my house. Indeed, from all I hear, I shouldn't like to.

[*Enter* mason.]

lady chiltern. What sort of a brooch was it that you lost, Mrs. Cheveley?

mrs. cheveley. A diamond snake-brooch with a ruby, a rather large ruby.

lady markby. I thought you said there was a sapphire on the head, dear?

mrs. cheveley [Smiling.] No, lady Markby—a ruby.

lady markby. [Nodding her head.] And very becoming, I am quite sure.

lady chiltern. Has a ruby and diamond brooch been found in any of the rooms this morning, Mason?

mason. No, my lady.

mrs. cheveley. It really is of no consequence, Lady Chiltern. I am so sorry to have put you to any inconvenience.

lady chiltern. [Coldly.] Oh, it has been no inconvenience. That will do, Mason. You can bring tea.

[*Exit* mason.]

lady markby. Well, I must say it is most annoying to lose anything. I remember once at Bath, years ago, losing in the Pump Room an exceedingly handsome cameo bracelet that Sir John had given me. I don't think he has ever given me anything since, I am sorry to say. He has sadly degenerated. Really, this horrid House of Commons quite ruins our husbands for us. I think the Lower House by far the greatest blow to a happy married life that there has been since that terrible thing called the Higher Education of Women was invented.

lady chiltern. Ah! it is heresy to say that in this house, Lady Markby. Robert is a great champion of the Higher Education of Women, and so, I am afraid, am I.

mrs. cheveley. The higher education of men is what I should like to see. Men need it so sadly.

lady markby. They do, dear. But I am afraid such a scheme would be quite unpractical. I don't think man has much capacity for development. He has got as far as he can, and that is not far, is it? With regard to women, well, dear Gertrude, you belong to the younger generation, and I am sure it is all right if you approve of it. In my time, of course, we were taught not to understand anything. That was the old system, and wonderfully interesting it was. I assure you that the amount of things I and my poor dear sister were taught not to understand was quite extraordinary. But modern women understand everything, I am told.

mrs. cheveley. Except their husbands. That is the one thing the modern woman never understands.

lady markby. And a very good thing too, dear, I dare say. It might break up many a happy home if they did. Not yours, I need hardly say, Gertrude. You have married a pattern husband. I wish I could say as much for myself. But since Sir John has taken to attending the debates regularly, which he never used to do in the good old days, his language has become quite impossible. He always seems to think that he is addressing the House, and consequently whenever he discusses the state of the agricultural labourer, or the Welsh Church, or something quite improper of that kind, I am obliged to send all the servants out of the room. It is not pleasant to see one's own butler, who has been with one for twenty-three years, actually blushing at the side-board, and the footmen making contortions in corners like persons in circuses. I assure you my life will be quite ruined unless they send John at once to the Upper House. He won't take any interest in politics then, will he? The House of Lords is so sensible. An assembly of gentlemen. But in his present state, Sir John is really a great trial. Why, this morning before breakfast was half over, he stood up on the hearthrug, put his hands in his pockets, and appealed to the country at the top of his voice. I left the table as soon as I had my second cup of tea, I need hardly say. But his violent language could be heard all over the house! I trust, Gertrude, that Sir Robert is not like that?

lady chiltern. But I am very much interested in politics, Lady Markby. I love to hear Robert talk about them.

lady markby. Well, I hope he is not as devoted to Blue Books as Sir John is. I don't think they can be quite improving reading for any one.

mrs. cheveley [Languidly.] I have never read a Blue Book. I prefer books . . . in yellow covers.

lady markby. [Genially unconscious.] Yellow is a gayer colour, is it not? I used to wear yellow a good deal in my early days, and would do so now if Sir John was not so painfully personal in his observations, and a man on the question of dress is always ridiculous, is he not?

mrs. cheveley. Oh, no! I think men are the only authorities on dress.

lady markby. Really? One wouldn't say so from the sort of hats they wear? would one?

[*The butler enters, followed by the footman. Tea is set on a small table close to l*ady chiltern.]

lady chiltern. May I give you some tea, Mrs. Cheveley?

mrs. cheveley. Thanks. [The butler hands mrs. cheveley a cup of tea on a salver.]

lady chiltern. Some tea, Lady Markby?

lady markby. No thanks, dear. [The servants go out.] The fact is, I have promised to go round for ten minutes to see poor Lady Brancaster, who is in very great trouble. Her daughter, quite a well-brought-up girl, too, has actually become engaged to be married to a curate in Shropshire. It is very sad, very sad indeed. I can't understand this modern mania for curates. In my time we girls saw them, of course, running about the place like rabbits. But we never took any notice of them, I need hardly say. But I am told that nowadays country society is quite honeycombed with them. I think it most irreligious. And then the eldest son has quarrelled with his father, and it is said that when they meet at the club Lord Brancaster always hides himself behind the money article in The Times. However, I believe that is quite a common occurrence nowadays and that they have to take in extra copies of The Times at all the clubs in St. James's Street; there are so many sons who won't have anything to do with their fathers, and so many fathers who won't speak to their sons. I think myself, it is very much to be regretted.

mrs. cheveley. So do I. Fathers have so much to learn from their sons nowadays.

lady markby. Really, dear? What?

mrs. cheveley. The art of living. The only really Fine Art we have produced in modern times.

lady markby. [Shaking her head.] Ah! I am afraid Lord Brancaster knew a good deal about that. More than his poor wife ever did. [Turning to lady chiltern.] You know Lady Brancaster, don't you, dear?

lady chiltern. Just slightly. She was staying at Langton last autumn, when we were there.

lady markby. Well, like all stout women, she looks the very picture of happiness, as no doubt you noticed. But there are many tragedies in her family, besides this affair of the curate. Her own sister, Mrs. Jekyll, had a most unhappy life; through no fault of her own, I am sorry to say. She ultimately was so broken-hearted that she went into a convent, or on to the operatic stage, I forget which. No; I think it was decorative art-needlework she took up. I know she had lost all sense of pleasure in life. [Rising.] And now, Gertrude, if you will allow me, I shall leave Mrs. Cheveley in your charge and call back for her in a quarter of an hour. Or perhaps, dear Mrs. Cheveley, you wouldn't mind waiting in the carriage while I am with Lady Brancaster. As I intend it to be a visit of condolence, I shan't stay long.

mrs. cheveley [Rising.] I don't mind waiting in the carriage at all, provided there is somebody to look at one.

lady markby. Well, I hear the curate is always prowling about the house.

mrs. cheveley. I am afraid I am not fond of girl friends.

lady chiltern [Rising.] Oh, I hope Mrs. Cheveley will stay here a little. I should like to have a few minutes' conversation with her.

mrs. cheveley. How very kind of you, Lady Chiltern! Believe me, nothing would give me greater pleasure.

lady markby. Ah! no doubt you both have many pleasant reminiscences of your schooldays to talk over together. Good-bye, dear Gertrude! Shall I see you at Lady Bonar's to-night? She has discovered a wonderful new genius. He does . . . nothing at all, I believe. That is a great comfort, is it not?

lady chiltern. Robert and I are dining at home by ourselves to-night, and I don't think I shall go anywhere afterwards. Robert, of course, will have to be in the House. But there is nothing interesting on.

lady markby. Dining at home by yourselves? Is that quite prudent?

Ah, I forgot, your husband is an exception. Mine is the general rule, and nothing ages a woman so rapidly as having married the general rule. [Exit lady markby.]

mrs. cheveley. Wonderful woman, Lady Markby, isn't she? Talks more and says less than anybody I ever met. She is made to be a public speaker. Much more so than her husband, though he is a typical Englishman, always dull and usually violent.

lady chiltern. [Makes no answer, but remains standing. There is a pause. Then the eyes of the two women meet. lady chiltern looks stern and pale. mrs. cheveley seem rather amused.] Mrs. Cheveley, I think it is right to tell you quite frankly that, had I known who you really were, I should not have invited you to my house last night.

mrs. cheveley [With an impertinent smile.] Really?

lady chiltern. I could not have done so.

mrs. cheveley. I see that after all these years you have not changed a bit, Gertrude.

lady chiltern. I never change.

mrs. cheveley [Elevating her eyebrows.] Then life has taught you nothing?

lady chiltern. It has taught me that a person who has once been guilty of a dishonest and dishonourable action may be guilty of it a second time, and should be shunned.

mrs. cheveley. Would you apply that rule to every one?

lady chiltern, Yes, to every one, without exception.

mrs. cheveley. Then I am sorry for you, Gertrude, very sorry for you.

lady chiltern. You see now, I was sure, that for many reasons any further acquaintance between us during your stay in London is quite impossible?

mrs. cheveley [Leaning back in her chair.] Do you know, Gertrude, I

71

don't mind your talking morality a bit. Morality is simply the attitude we adopt towards people whom we personally dislike. You dislike me. I am quite aware of that. And I have always detested you. And yet I have come here to do you a service.

lady chiltern. [Contemptuously.] Like the service you wished to render my husband last night, I suppose. Thank heaven, I saved him from that.

mrs. cheveley. [Starting to her feet.] It was you who made him write that insolent letter to me? It was you who made him break his promise?

lady chiltern. Yes.

mrs. cheveley. Then you must make him keep it. I give you till to-morrow morning—no more. If by that time your husband does not solemnly bind himself to help me in this great scheme in which I am interested—

lady chiltern. This fraudulent speculation—

mrs. cheveley. Call it what you choose. I hold your husband in the hollow of my hand, and if you are wise you will make him do what I tell him.

lady chiltern. [Rising and going towards her.] You are impertinent. What has my husband to do with you? With a woman like you?

mrs. cheveley [With a bitter laugh.] In this world like meets with like. It is because your husband is himself fraudulent and dishonest that we pair so well together. Between you and him there are chasms. He and I are closer than friends. We are enemies linked together. The same sin binds us.

lady chiltern. How dare you class my husband with yourself? How dare you threaten him or me? Leave my house. You are unfit to enter it.

[sir robert chiltern enters from behind. He hears his wife's last words, and sees to whom they are addressed. He grows deadly pale.]

mrs. cheveley. Your house! A house bought with the price of dishonour. A house, everything in which has been paid for by fraud. [Turns round and sees sir robert chiltern.] Ask him what the origin of his fortune is! Get him to tell you how he sold to a stockbroker a Cabinet secret. Learn from him to what you owe your position.

lady chiltern. It is not true! Robert! It is not true!

mrs. cheveley. [Pointing at him with outstretched finger.] Look at him! Can he deny it? Does he dare to?

sir robert chiltern. Go! Go at once. You have done your worst now.

mrs. cheveley. My worst? I have not yet finished with you, with either of you. I give you both till to-morrow at noon. If by then you don't do what I bid you to do, the whole world shall know the origin of Robert Chiltern.

[sir robert chiltern strikes the bell. Enter mason.]

sir robert chiltern. Show Mrs. Cheveley out.

[mrs. cheveley *starts; then bows with somewhat exaggerated politeness to* lady chiltern, *who makes no sign of response. As she passes by* sir robert chiltern, *who is standing close to the door, she pauses for a moment and looks him straight in the face. She then goes out, followed by the servant, who closes the door after him. The husband and wife are left alone.* lady chiltern *stands like some one in a dreadful dream. Then she turns round and looks at her husband. She looks at him with strange eyes, as though she were seeing him for the first time.*]

lady chiltern. You sold a Cabinet secret for money! You began your life with fraud! You built up your career on dishonour! Oh, tell me it is not true! Lie to me! Lie to me! Tell me it is not true!

sir robert chiltern. What this woman said is quite true. But, Gertrude, listen to me. You don't realise how I was tempted. Let me tell you the whole thing. [Goes towards her.]

lady chiltern. Don't come near me. Don't touch me. I feel as if you had soiled me for ever. Oh! what a mask you have been wearing all these years! A horrible painted mask! You sold yourself for money. Oh! a common thief were better. You put yourself up to sale to the highest bidder! You were bought in the market. You lied to the whole world. And yet you will not lie to me.

sir robert chiltern. [Rushing towards her.] Gertrude! Gertrude!

lady chiltern. [Thrusting him back with outstretched hands.] No, don't speak! Say nothing! Your voice wakes terrible memories—memories of things that made me love you—memories of words that made me love you—memories that now are horrible to me. And how I worshipped you! You were to me something apart from common life, a thing pure, noble, honest, without stain. The world seemed to me finer because you were in it, and goodness more real because you lived. And now—oh, when I think that I made of a man like you my ideal! the ideal of my life!

sir robert chiltern. There was your mistake. There was your error. The error all women commit. Why can't you women love us, faults and all? Why do you place us on monstrous pedestals? We have all feet of clay, women as well as men; but when we men love women, we love them knowing their weaknesses, their follies, their imperfections, love them all the more, it may be, for that reason. It is not the perfect, but the imperfect, who have need of love. It is when we are wounded by our own hands, or by the hands of others, that love should come to cure us—else what use is love at all? All sins, except a sin against itself, Love should forgive. All lives, save loveless lives, true Love should pardon. A man's love is like that. It is wider, larger, more human than a woman's. Women think that they are making ideals of men. What they are making of us are false idols merely. You made your false idol of me, and I had not the courage to come down, show you my wounds, tell you my weaknesses. I was afraid that I might lose your love, as I have lost it now. And so, last night you ruined my life for me—yes, ruined it! What this woman asked of me was nothing compared to what she offered to me. She offered security, peace, stability. The sin of my youth, that I had thought was buried, rose up in front of me, hideous, horrible, with its hands at my throat. I could have killed it for ever, sent it back into its tomb, destroyed its record, burned the one witness against me. You prevented me. No one but you, you know it. And now what is there before me but public disgrace, ruin, terrible shame, the mockery of the world, a lonely dishonoured life, a lonely dishonoured death, it may be, some day? Let women make no more ideals of men! let them not put them on alters and bow before them, or they may ruin other lives as completely as you—you whom I have so wildly loved—have ruined mine!

[*He passes from the room.* lady chiltern *rushes towards him, but the door is closed when she reaches it. Pale with anguish, bewildered, helpless, she sways like a plant in the water. Her hands, outstretched, seem to tremble in the air like blossoms in the mind. Then she flings herself down beside a sofa and buries her face. Her sobs are like the sobs of a child.*]

Act Drop

THIRD ACT

SCENE

The Library in Lord Goring's house. An Adam room. On the right is the door leading into the hall. On the left, the door of the smoking-room. A pair of folding doors at the back open into the drawing-room. The fire is lit. Phipps, the butler, is arranging some newspapers on the writing-table. The distinction of Phipps is his impassivity. He has been termed by enthusiasts the Ideal Butler. The Sphinx is not so incommunicable. He is a mask with a manner. Of his intellectual or emotional life, history knows nothing. He represents the dominance of form.

[Enter lord goring *in evening dress with a buttonhole. He is wearing a silk hat and Inverness cape. White-gloved, he carries a Louis Seize cane. His are all the delicate fopperies of Fashion. One sees that he stands in immediate relation to modern life, makes it indeed, and so masters it. He is the first well-dressed philosopher in the history of thought.]*

lord goring. Got my second buttonhole for me, Phipps?

phipps. Yes, my lord. [Takes his hat, cane, and cape, and presents new buttonhole on salver.]

lord goring. Rather distinguished thing, Phipps. I am the only person of the smallest importance in London at present who wears a buttonhole.

phipps. Yes, my lord. I have observed that,

lord goring. [Taking out old buttonhole.] You see, Phipps, Fashion is what one wears oneself. What is unfashionable is what other people wear.

phipps. Yes, my lord.

lord goring. Just as vulgarity is simply the conduct of other people.

phipps. Yes, my lord.

lord goring. [Putting in a new buttonhole.] And falsehoods the truths of other people.

phipps. Yes, my lord.

lord goring. Other people are quite dreadful. The only possible society is oneself.

phipps. Yes, my lord.

lord goring. To love oneself is the beginning of a lifelong romance, Phipps.

phipps. Yes, my lord.

lord goring. [Looking at himself in the glass.] Don't think I quite like this buttonhole, Phipps. Makes me look a little too old. Makes me almost in the prime of life, eh, Phipps?

phipps. I don't observe any alteration in your lordship's appearance.

lord goring. You don't, Phipps?

phipps. No, my lord.

lord goring. I am not quite sure. For the future a more trivial buttonhole, Phipps, on Thursday evenings.

phipps. I will speak to the florist, my lord. She has had a loss in her family lately, which perhaps accounts for the lack of triviality your lordship complains of in the buttonhole.

lord goring. Extraordinary thing about the lower classes in England—they are always losing their relations.

phipps. Yes, my lord! They are extremely fortunate in that respect.

lord goring. [Turns round and looks at him. phipps remains impassive.] Hum! Any letters, Phipps?

phipps. Three, my lord. [Hands letters on a salver.]

lord goring. [Takes letters.] Want my cab round in twenty minutes.

phipps. Yes, my lord. [Goes towards door.]

lord goring. [Holds up letter in pink envelope.] Ahem! Phipps, when did this letter arrive?

phipps. It was brought by hand just after your lordship went to the club.

lord goring. That will do. [Exit phipps.] Lady Chiltern's handwriting on Lady Chiltern's pink notepaper. That is rather curious. I thought Robert was to write. Wonder what Lady Chiltern has got to say to me? [Sits at bureau and opens letter, and reads it.] 'I want you. I trust you. I am coming to you. Gertrude.' [Puts down the letter with a puzzled look. Then takes it up, and reads it again slowly.] 'I want you. I trust you. I am coming to you.' So she has found out everything! Poor woman! Poor woman! [Pulls out watch and looks at it.] But what an hour to call! Ten o'clock! I shall have to give up going to the Berkshires. However, it is always nice to be expected, and not to arrive. I am not expected at the Bachelors', so I shall certainly go there. Well, I will make her stand by her husband. That is the only thing for her to do. That is the only thing for any woman to do. It is the growth of the moral sense in women that makes marriage such a hopeless, one-sided institution. Ten o'clock. She should be here soon. I must tell Phipps I am not in to any one else. [Goes towards bell]

[*Enter* phipps.]

phipps. Lord Caversham.

lord goring. Oh, why will parents always appear at the wrong time? Some extraordinary mistake in nature, I suppose. [Enter lord caversham.] Delighted to see you, my dear father. [Goes to meet him.]

lord caversham. Take my cloak off.

lord goring. Is it worth while, father?

lord caversham. Of course it is worth while, sir. Which is the most comfortable chair?

lord goring. This one, father. It is the chair I use myself, when I have visitors.

lord caversham. Thank ye. No draught, I hope, in this room?

lord goring. No, father.

lord caversham. [Sitting down.] Glad to hear it. Can't stand draughts. No draughts at home.

lord goring. Good many breezes, father.

lord caversham. Eh? Eh? Don't understand what you mean. Want to have a serious conversation with you, sir.

lord goring. My dear father! At this hour?

lord caversham. Well, sir, it is only ten o'clock. What is your objection to the hour? I think the hour is an admirable hour!

lord goring. Well, the fact is, father, this is not my day for talking seriously. I am very sorry, but it is not my day.

lord caversham. What do you mean, sir?

lord goring. During the Season, father, I only talk seriously on the first Tuesday in every month, from four to seven.

lord caversham. Well, make it Tuesday, sir, make it Tuesday.

lord goring. But it is after seven, father, and my doctor says I must not have any serious conversation after seven. It makes me talk in my sleep.

lord caversham. Talk in your sleep, sir? What does that matter? You are not married.

lord goring. No, father, I am not married.

lord caversham. Hum! That is what I have come to talk to you about, sir. You have got to get married, and at once. Why, when I was your age, sir, I had been an inconsolable widower for three months, and was already paying my addresses to your admirable mother. Damme, sir, it is your duty to get married. You can't be always living for pleasure. Every man of position is married nowadays. Bachelors are not fashionable any more. They are a damaged lot. Too much is known about them. You must get a wife, sir. Look where your friend Robert Chiltern has got to by probity, hard work, and a sensible marriage with a good woman. Why don't you imitate him, sir? Why don't you take him for your model?

lord goring. I think I shall, father.

lord caversham. I wish you would, sir. Then I should be happy. At present I make your mother's life miserable on your account. You are heartless, sir, quite heartless.

lord goring. I hope not, father.

lord caversham. And it is high time for you to get married. You are thirty-four years of age, sir.

lord goring. Yes, father, but I only admit to thirty-two—thirty-one and a half when I have a really good buttonhole. This buttonhole is not . . . trivial enough.

lord caversham. I tell you you are thirty-four, sir. And there is a draught in your room, besides, which makes your conduct worse. Why did you tell me there was no draught, sir? I feel a draught, sir, I feel it distinctly.

lord goring. So do I, father. It is a dreadful draught. I will come and see you to-morrow, father. We can talk over anything you like. Let me help you on with your cloak, father.

lord caversham. No, sir; I have called this evening for a definite purpose, and I am going to see it through at all costs to my health or yours. Put down my cloak, sir.

lord goring. Certainly, father. But let us go into another room. [Rings bell.] There is a dreadful draught here. [Enter phipps.] Phipps, is there a good fire in the smoking-room?

phipps. Yes, my lord.

lord goring. Come in there, father. Your sneezes are quite heartrending.

80

lord caversham. Well, sir, I suppose I have a right to sneeze when I choose?

lord goring. [Apologetically.] Quite so, father. I was merely expressing sympathy.

lord caversham. Oh, damn sympathy. There is a great deal too much of that sort of thing going on nowadays.

lord goring. I quite agree with you, father. If there was less sympathy in the world there would be less trouble in the world.

lord caversham. [Going towards the smoking-room.] That is a paradox, sir. I hate paradoxes.

lord goring. So do I, father. Everybody one meets is a paradox nowadays. It is a great bore. It makes society so obvious.

lord caversham. [Turning round, and looking at his son beneath his bushy eyebrows.] Do you always really understand what you say, sir?

lord goring. [After some hesitation.] Yes, father, if I listen attentively.

lord caversham. [Indignantly.] If you listen attentively! . . . Conceited young puppy!

[*Goes off grumbling into the smoking-room.* phipps *enters.*]

lord goring. Phipps, there is a lady coming to see me this evening on particular business. Show her into the drawing-room when she arrives. You understand?

phipps. Yes, my lord.

lord goring. It is a matter of the gravest importance, Phipps.

phipps. I understand, my lord.

lord goring. No one else is to be admitted, under any circumstances.

phipps. I understand, my lord. [Bell rings.]

lord goring. Ah! that is probably the lady. I shall see her myself.

[*Just as he is going towards the door* lord caversham *enters from the smoking-room.*]

lord caversham. Well, sir? am I to wait attendance on you?

lord goring. [Considerably perplexed.] In a moment, father. Do excuse me. [lord caversham goes back.] Well, remember my instructions, Phipps—into that room.

phipps. Yes, my lord.

[lord goring *goes into the smoking-room.* harold, *the footman shows* mrs. cheveley *in. Lamia-like, she is in green and silver. She has a cloak of black satin, lined with dead rose-leaf silk.*]

harold. What name, madam?

mrs. cheveley. [To phipps, who advances towards her.] Is Lord Goring not here? I was told he was at home?

phipps. His lordship is engaged at present with Lord Caversham, madam.

[*Turns a cold, glassy eye on* harold, *who at once retires.*]

mrs. cheveley. [To herself.] How very filial!

phipps. His lordship told me to ask you, madam, to be kind enough to wait in the drawing-room for him. His lordship will come to you there.

mrs. cheveley. [With a look of surprise.] Lord Goring expects me?

phipps. Yes, madam.

mrs. cheveley. Are you quite sure?

phipps. His lordship told me that if a lady called I was to ask her to wait in the drawing-room. [Goes to the door of the drawing-room and opens it.] His lordship's directions on the subject were very precise.

mrs. cheveley. [To herself] How thoughtful of him! To expect the unexpected shows a thoroughly modern intellect. [Goes towards the drawing-room and looks in.] Ugh! How dreary a bachelor's drawing-room always looks. I shall have to alter all this. [phipps brings the lamp from the writing-table.] No, I don't care for that lamp. It is far too glaring. Light some candles.

phipps. [Replaces lamp.] Certainly, madam.

mrs. cheveley. I hope the candles have very becoming shades.

phipps. We have had no complaints about them, madam, as yet.

[*Passes into the drawing-room and begins to light the candles.*]

mrs. cheveley. [To herself.] I wonder what woman he is waiting for to-night. It will be delightful to catch him. Men always look so silly when they are caught. And they are always being caught. [Looks about room and approaches the writing-table.] What a very interesting room! What a very interesting picture! Wonder what his correspondence is like. [Takes up letters.] Oh, what a very uninteresting correspondence! Bills and cards, debts and dowagers! Who on earth writes to him on pink paper? How silly to write on pink paper! It looks like the beginning of a middle-class romance. Romance should never begin with sentiment. It should begin with science and end with a settlement. [Puts letter down, then takes it up again.] I know that handwriting. That is Gertrude Chiltern's. I remember it perfectly. The ten commandments in every stroke of the pen, and the moral law all over the page. Wonder what Gertrude is writing to him about? Something horrid about me, I suppose. How I detest that woman! [Reads it.] 'I trust you. I want you. I am coming to you. Gertrude.' 'I trust you. I want you. I am coming to you.'

[*A look of triumph comes over her face. She is just about to steal the letter, when* phipps *comes in.*]

phipps. The candles in the drawing-room are lit, madam, as you directed.

mrs. cheveley. Thank you. [Rises hastily and slips the letter under a large silver-cased blotting-book that is lying on the table.]

phipps. I trust the shades will be to your liking, madam. They are the most becoming we have. They are the same as his lordship uses himself when he is dressing for dinner.

mrs. cheveley. [With a smile.] Then I am sure they will be perfectly right.

phipps. [Gravely.] Thank you, madam.

[mrs. cheveley *goes into the drawing-room.* phipps *closes the door and retires. The door is then slowly opened, and* mrs. cheveley *comes out and creeps stealthily towards the writing-table. Suddenly voices are heard from the smoking-room.* mrs. cheveley *grows pale, and stops. The voices grow louder, and she goes back into the drawing-room, biting her lip.*]

[*Enter* lord goring *and* lord caversham.]

lord goring. [Expostulating.] My dear father, if I am to get married, surely you will allow me to choose the time, place, and person? Particularly the person.

lord caversham. [Testily.] That is a matter for me, sir. You would probably make a very poor choice. It is I who should be consulted, not you. There is property at stake. It is not a matter for affection. Affection comes later on in married life.

lord goring. Yes. In married life affection comes when people thoroughly dislike each other, father, doesn't it? [Puts on lord caversham's cloak for him.]

lord caversham. Certainly, sir. I mean certainly not, air. You are talking very foolishly to-night. What I say is that marriage is a matter for common sense.

lord goring. But women who have common sense are so curiously plain, father, aren't they? Of course I only speak from hearsay.

lord caversham. No woman, plain or pretty, has any common sense at all, sir. Common sense is the privilege of our sex.

lord goring. Quite so. And we men are so self-sacrificing that we never

84

use it, do we, father?

lord caversham. I use it, sir. I use nothing else.

lord goring. So my mother tells me.

lord caversham. It is the secret of your mother's happiness. You are very heartless, sir, very heartless.

lord goring. I hope not, father.

[*Goes out for a moment. Then returns, looking rather put out, with* sir robert chiltern.]

sir robert chiltern. My dear Arthur, what a piece of good luck meeting you on the doorstep! Your servant had just told me you were not at home. How extraordinary!

lord goring. The fact is, I am horribly busy to-night, Robert, and I gave orders I was not at home to any one. Even my father had a comparatively cold reception. He complained of a draught the whole time.

sir robert chiltern. Ah! you must be at home to me, Arthur. You are my best friend. Perhaps by to-morrow you will be my only friend. My wife has discovered everything.

lord goring. Ah! I guessed as much!

sir robert chiltern. [Looking at him.] Really! How?

lord goring. [After some hesitation.] Oh, merely by something in the expression of your face as you came in. Who told her?

sir robert chiltern. Mrs. Cheveley herself. And the woman I love knows that I began my career with an act of low dishonesty, that I built up my life upon sands of shame—that I sold, like a common huckster, the secret that had been intrusted to me as a man of honour. I thank heaven poor Lord Radley died without knowing that I betrayed him. I would to God I had died before I had been so horribly tempted, or had fallen so low. [Burying his face in his hands.]

lord goring. [After a pause.] You have heard nothing from Vienna yet, in answer to your wire?

sir robert chiltern. [Looking up.] Yes; I got a telegram from the first secretary at eight o'clock to-night.

lord goring. Well?

sir robert chiltern. Nothing is absolutely known against her. On the contrary, she occupies a rather high position in society. It is a sort of open secret that Baron Arnheim left her the greater portion of his immense fortune. Beyond that I can learn nothing.

lord goring. She doesn't turn out to be a spy, then?

sir robert chiltern. Oh! spies are of no use nowadays. Their profession is over. The newspapers do their work instead.

lord goring. And thunderingly well they do it.

sir robert chiltern. Arthur, I am parched with thirst. May I ring for something? Some hock and seltzer?

lord goring. Certainly. Let me. [Rings the bell.]

sir robert chiltern. Thanks! I don't know what to do, Arthur, I don't know what to do, and you are my only friend. But what a friend you are— the one friend I can trust. I can trust you absolutely, can't I?

[*Enter* phipps.]

lord goring. My dear Robert, of course. Oh! [To phipps.] Bring some hock and seltzer.

phipps. Yes, my lord.

lord goring. And Phipps!

phipps. Yes, my lord.

lord goring. Will you excuse me for a moment, Robert? I want to give some directions to my servant.

sir robert chiltern. Certainly.

lord goring. When that lady calls, tell her that I am not expected home this evening. Tell her that I have been suddenly called out of town. You understand?

phipps. The lady is in that room, my lord. You told me to show her into that room, my lord.

lord goring. You did perfectly right. [Exit phipps.] What a mess I am in. No; I think I shall get through it. I'll give her a lecture through the door. Awkward thing to manage, though.

sir robert chiltern. Arthur, tell me what I should do. My life seems to have crumbled about me. I am a ship without a rudder in a night without a star.

lord goring. Robert, you love your wife, don't you?

sir robert chiltern. I love her more than anything in the world. I used to think ambition the great thing. It is not. Love is the great thing in the world. There is nothing but love, and I love her. But I am defamed in her eyes. I am ignoble in her eyes. There is a wide gulf between us now. She has found me out, Arthur, she has found me out.

lord goring. Has she never in her life done some folly—some indiscretion—that she should not forgive your sin?

sir robert chiltern. My wife! Never! She does not know what weakness or temptation is. I am of clay like other men. She stands apart as good women do—pitiless in her perfection—cold and stern and without mercy. But I love her, Arthur. We are childless, and I have no one else to love, no one else to love me. Perhaps if God had sent us children she might have been kinder to me. But God has given us a lonely house. And she has cut my heart in two. Don't let us talk of it. I was brutal to her this evening. But I suppose when sinners talk to saints they are brutal always. I said to her things that were hideously true, on my side, from my stand-point, from the standpoint of men. But don't let us talk of that.

lord goring. Your wife will forgive you. Perhaps at this moment she is forgiving you. She loves you, Robert. Why should she not forgive?

sir robert chiltern. God grant it! God grant it! [Buries his face in his hands.] But there is something more I have to tell you, Arthur.

[*Enter* phipps *with drinks.*]

phipps. [Hands hock and seltzer to sir robert chiltern.] Hock and seltzer, sir.

sir robert chiltern. Thank you.

lord goring. Is your carriage here, Robert?

sir robert chiltern. No; I walked from the club.

lord goring. Sir Robert will take my cab, Phipps.

phipps. Yes, my lord. [Exit.]

lord goring. Robert, you don't mind my sending you away?

sir robert chiltern. Arthur, you must let me stay for five minutes. I have made up my mind what I am going to do to-night in the House. The debate on the Argentine Canal is to begin at eleven. [A chair falls in the drawing-room.] What is that?

lord goring. Nothing.

sir robert chiltern. I heard a chair fall in the next room. Some one has been listening.

lord goring. No, no; there is no one there.

sir robert chiltern. There is some one. There are lights in the room, and the door is ajar. Some one has been listening to every secret of my life. Arthur, what does this mean?

lord goring. Robert, you are excited, unnerved. I tell you there is no one in that room. Sit down, Robert.

sir robert chiltern. Do you give me your word that there is no one there?

lord goring. Yes.

sir robert chiltern. Your word of honour? [Sits down.]

lord goring. Yes.

sir robert chiltern. [Rises.] Arthur, let me see for myself.

lord goring. No, no.

sir robert chiltern. If there is no one there why should I not look in that room? Arthur, you must let me go into that room and satisfy myself. Let me know that no eavesdropper has heard my life's secret. Arthur, you don't realise what I am going through.

lord goring. Robert, this must stop. I have told you that there is no one in that room—that is enough.

sir robert chiltern. [Rushes to the door of the room.] It is not enough. I insist on going into this room. You have told me there is no one there, so what reason can you have for refusing me?

lord goring. For God's sake, don't! There is some one there. Some one whom you must not see.

sir robert chiltern. Ah, I thought so!

lord goring. I forbid you to enter that room.

sir robert chiltern. Stand back. My life is at stake. And I don't care who is there. I will know who it is to whom I have told my secret and my shame. [Enters room.]

lord goring. Great heavens! his own wife!

[sir robert chiltern *comes back, with a look of scorn and anger on his face.*]

sir robert chiltern. What explanation have you to give me for the presence of that woman here?

lord goring. Robert, I swear to you on my honour that that lady is stainless and guiltless of all offence towards you.

sir robert chiltern. She is a vile, an infamous thing!

lord goring. Don't say that, Robert! It was for your sake she came here. It was to try and save you she came here. She loves you and no one else.

sir robert chiltern. You are mad. What have I to do with her intrigues with you? Let her remain your mistress! You are well suited to each other. She, corrupt and shameful—you, false as a friend, treacherous as an enemy even—

lord goring. It is not true, Robert. Before heaven, it is not true. In her presence and in yours I will explain all.

sir robert chiltern. Let me pass, sir. You have lied enough upon your word of honour.

[sir robert chiltern *goes out.* lord goring *rushes to the door of the drawing-room, when* mrs. cheveley *comes out, looking radiant and much amused.*]

mrs. cheveley. [With a mock curtsey] Good evening, Lord Goring!

lord goring. Mrs. Cheveley! Great heavens! . . . May I ask what you were doing in my drawing-room?

mrs. cheveley. Merely listening. I have a perfect passion for listening through keyholes. One always hears such wonderful things through them.

lord goring. Doesn't that sound rather like tempting Providence?

mrs. cheveley. Oh! surely Providence can resist temptation by this time. [Makes a sign to him to take her cloak off, which he does.]

lord goring. I am glad you have called. I am going to give you some good advice.

mrs. cheveley. Oh! pray don't. One should never give a woman anything that she can't wear in the evening.

lord goring. I see you are quite as wilful as you used to be.

mrs. cheveley. Far more! I have greatly improved. I have had more experience.

lord goring. Too much experience is a dangerous thing. Pray have a cigarette. Half the pretty women in London smoke cigarettes. Personally I prefer the other half.

mrs. cheveley. Thanks. I never smoke. My dressmaker wouldn't like it, and a woman's first duty in life is to her dressmaker, isn't it? What the second duty is, no one has as yet discovered.

lord goring. You have come here to sell me Robert Chiltern's letter, haven't you?

mrs. cheveley. To offer it to you on conditions. How did you guess that?

lord goring. Because you haven't mentioned the subject. Have you got it with you?

mrs. cheveley. [Sitting down.] Oh, no! A well-made dress has no pockets.

lord goring. What is your price for it?

mrs. cheveley. How absurdly English you are! The English think that a cheque-book can solve every problem in life. Why, my dear Arthur, I have very much more money than you have, and quite as much as Robert Chiltern has got hold of. Money is not what I want.

lord goring. What do you want then, Mrs. Cheveley?

mrs. cheveley. Why don't you call me Laura?

lord goring. I don't like the name.

mrs. cheveley. You used to adore it.

lord goring. Yes: that's why. [mrs. cheveley motions to him to sit down beside her. He smiles, and does so.]

mrs. cheveley. Arthur, you loved me once.

lord goring. Yes.

mrs. cheveley. And you asked me to be your wife.

lord goring. That was the natural result of my loving you.

mrs. cheveley. And you threw me over because you saw, or said you saw, poor old Lord Mortlake trying to have a violent flirtation with me in the conservatory at Tenby.

lord goring. I am under the impression that my lawyer settled that matter with you on certain terms . . . dictated by yourself.

mrs. cheveley. At that time I was poor; you were rich.

lord goring. Quite so. That is why you pretended to love me.

mrs. cheveley. [Shrugging her shoulders.] Poor old Lord Mortlake, who had only two topics of conversation, his gout and his wife! I never could quite make out which of the two he was talking about. He used the most horrible language about them both. Well, you were silly, Arthur. Why, Lord Mortlake was never anything more to me than an amusement. One of those utterly tedious amusements one only finds at an English country house on an English country Sunday. I don't think any one at all morally responsible for what he or she does at an English country house.

lord goring. Yes. I know lots of people think that.

mrs. cheveley. I loved you, Arthur.

lord goring. My dear Mrs. Cheveley, you have always been far too clever to know anything about love.

mrs. cheveley. I did love you. And you loved me. You know you loved me; and love is a very wonderful thing. I suppose that when a man has once loved a woman, he will do anything for her, except continue to love her? [Puts her hand on his.]

lord goring. [Taking his hand away quietly.] Yes: except that.

mrs. cheveley. [After a pause.] I am tired of living abroad. I want to

92

come back to London. I want to have a charming house here. I want to have a salon. If one could only teach the English how to talk, and the Irish how to listen, society here would be quite civilised. Besides, I have arrived at the romantic stage. When I saw you last night at the Chilterns', I knew you were the only person I had ever cared for, if I ever have cared for anybody, Arthur. And so, on the morning of the day you marry me, I will give you Robert Chiltern's letter. That is my offer. I will give it to you now, if you promise to marry me.

lord goring. Now?

mrs. cheveley. [Smiling.] To-morrow.

lord goring. Are you really serious?

mrs. cheveley. Yes, quite serious.

lord goring. I should make you a very bad husband.

mrs. cheveley. I don't mind bad husbands. I have had two. They amused me immensely.

lord goring. You mean that you amused yourself immensely, don't you?

mrs. cheveley. What do you know about my married life?

lord goring. Nothing: but I can read it like a book.

mrs. cheveley. What book?

lord goring. [Rising.] The Book of Numbers.

mrs. cheveley. Do you think it is quite charming of you to be so rude to a woman in your own house?

lord goring. In the case of very fascinating women, sex is a challenge, not a defence.

mrs. cheveley. I suppose that is meant for a compliment. My dear Arthur, women are never disarmed by compliments. Men always are. That is the difference between the two sexes.

lord goring. Women are never disarmed by anything, as far as I know them.

mrs. cheveley. [After a pause.] Then you are going to allow your greatest friend, Robert Chiltern, to be ruined, rather than marry some one who really has considerable attractions left. I thought you would have risen to some great height of self-sacrifice, Arthur. I think you should. And the rest of your life you could spend in contemplating your own perfections.

lord goring. Oh! I do that as it is. And self-sacrifice is a thing that should be put down by law. It is so demoralising to the people for whom one sacrifices oneself. They always go to the bad.

mrs. cheveley. As if anything could demoralise Robert Chiltern! You seem to forget that I know his real character.

lord goring. What you know about him is not his real character. It was an act of folly done in his youth, dishonourable, I admit, shameful, I admit, unworthy of him, I admit, and therefore . . . not his true character.

mrs. cheveley. How you men stand up for each other!

lord goring. How you women war against each other!

mrs. cheveley. [Bitterly.] I only war against one woman, against Gertrude Chiltern. I hate her. I hate her now more than ever.

lord goring. Because you have brought a real tragedy into her life, I suppose.

mrs. cheveley. [With a sneer.] Oh, there is only one real tragedy in a woman's life. The fact that her past is always her lover, and her future invariably her husband.

lord goring. Lady Chiltern knows nothing of the kind of life to which you are alluding.

mrs. cheveley. A woman whose size in gloves is seven and three-quarters never knows much about anything. You know Gertrude has always worn seven and three-quarters? That is one of the reasons why there was never any moral sympathy between us. . . . Well, Arthur, I suppose this romantic interview may be regarded as at an end. You admit it was romantic, don't you? For the privilege of being your wife I was ready to surrender a great prize, the climax of my diplomatic career. You decline. Very well. If Sir Robert doesn't uphold my Argentine scheme, I expose him. Voilà tout.

lord goring. You mustn't do that. It would be vile, horrible, infamous.

mrs. cheveley. [Shrugging her shoulders.] Oh! don't use big words. They mean so little. It is a commercial transaction. That is all. There is no good mixing up sentimentality in it. I offered to sell Robert Chiltern a certain thing. If he won't pay me my price, he will have to pay the world a greater price. There is no more to be said. I must go. Good-bye. Won't you shake hands?

lord goring. With you? No. Your transaction with Robert Chiltern may pass as a loathsome commercial transaction of a loathsome commercial age; but you seem to have forgotten that you came here to-night to talk of love, you whose lips desecrated the word love, you to whom the thing is a book closely sealed, went this afternoon to the house of one of the most noble and gentle women in the world to degrade her husband in her eyes, to try and kill her love for him, to put poison in her heart, and bitterness in her life, to break her idol, and, it may be, spoil her soul. That I cannot forgive you. That was horrible. For that there can be no forgiveness.

mrs. cheveley. Arthur, you are unjust to me. Believe me, you are quite unjust to me. I didn't go to taunt Gertrude at all. I had no idea of doing anything of the kind when I entered. I called with Lady Markby simply to ask whether an ornament, a jewel, that I lost somewhere last night, had been found at the Chilterns'. If you don't believe me, you can ask Lady Markby. She will tell you it is true. The scene that occurred happened after Lady Markby had left, and was really forced on me by Gertrude's rudeness and sneers. I called, oh!—a little out of malice if you like—but really to ask if a diamond brooch of mine had been found. That was the origin of the whole thing.

lord goring. A diamond snake-brooch with a ruby?

mrs. cheveley. Yes. How do you know?

lord goring. Because it is found. In point of fact, I found it myself, and stupidly forgot to tell the butler anything about it as I was leaving. [Goes over to the writing-table and pulls out the drawers.] It is in this drawer. No, that one. This is the brooch, isn't it? [Holds up the brooch.]

mrs. cheveley. Yes. I am so glad to get it back. It was . . a present.

lord goring. Won't you wear it?

mrs. cheveley. Certainly, if you pin it in. [lord goring suddenly clasps it on her arm.] Why do you put it on as a bracelet? I never knew it could he worn as a bracelet.

lord goring. Really?

mrs. cheveley. [Holding out her handsome arm.] No; but it looks very well on me as a bracelet, doesn't it?

lord goring. Yes; much better than when I saw it last.

mrs. cheveley. When did you see it last?

lord goring. [Calmly.] Oh, ten years ago, on Lady Berkshire, from whom you stole it.

mrs. cheveley. [Starting.] What do you mean?

lord goring. I mean that you stole that ornament from my cousin, Mary Berkshire, to whom I gave it when she was married. Suspicion fell on a wretched servant, who was sent away in disgrace. I recognised it last night. I determined to say nothing about it till I had found the thief. I have found the thief now, and I have heard her own confession.

mrs. cheveley. [Tossing her head.] It is not true.

lord goring. You know it is true. Why, thief is written across your face at this moment.

mrs. cheveley. I will deny the whole affair from beginning to end. I will say that I have never seen this wretched thing, that it was never in my possession.

[mrs. cheveley *tries to get the bracelet off her arm, but fails.* lord goring *looks on amused. Her thin fingers tear at the jewel to no purpose. A curse breaks from her.*]

lord goring. The drawback of stealing a thing, Mrs. Cheveley, is that one never knows how wonderful the thing that one steals is. You can't get that bracelet off, unless you know where the spring is. And I see you don't know where the spring is. It is rather difficult to find.

mrs. cheveley. You brute! You coward! [She tries again to unclasp the bracelet, but fails.]

lord goring. Oh! don't use big words. They mean so little.

mrs. cheveley. [Again tears at the bracelet in a paroxysm of rage, with inarticulate sounds. Then stops, and looks at lord goring.] What are you going to do?

lord goring. I am going to ring for my servant. He is an admirable servant. Always comes in the moment one rings for him. When he comes I will tell him to fetch the police.

mrs. cheveley. [Trembling.] The police? What for?

lord goring. To-morrow the Berkshires will prosecute you. That is what the police are for.

mrs. cheveley. [Is now in an agony of physical terror. Her face is distorted. Her mouth awry. A mask has fallen from her. She it, for the moment, dreadful to look at.] Don't do that. I will do anything you want. Anything in the world you want.

lord goring. Give me Robert Chiltern's letter.

mrs. cheveley. Stop! Stop! Let me have time to think.

lord goring. Give me Robert Chiltern's letter.

mrs. cheveley. I have not got it with me. I will give it to you to-morrow.

lord goring. You know you are lying. Give it to me at once. [mrs. cheveley pulls the letter out, and hands it to him. She is horribly pale.] This is it?

mrs. cheveley. [In a hoarse voice.] Yes.

lord goring. [Takes the letter, examines it, sighs, and burns it with the lamp.] For so well-dressed a woman, Mrs. Cheveley, you have moments of admirable common sense. I congratulate you.

mrs. cheveley. [Catches sight of lady chiltern's letter, the cover of which is just showing from under the blotting-book.] Please get me a glass of water.

lord goring. Certainly. [Goes to the corner of the room and pours out a glass of water. While his back is turned mrs. cheveley steals lady chiltern's letter. When lord goring returns the glass she refuses it with a gesture.]

mrs. cheveley. Thank you. Will you help me on with my cloak?

lord goring. With pleasure. [Puts her cloak on.]

mrs. cheveley. Thanks. I am never going to try to harm Robert Chiltern again.

lord goring. Fortunately you have not the chance, Mrs. Cheveley.

mrs. cheveley. Well, if even I had the chance, I wouldn't. On the contrary, I am going to render him a great service.

lord goring. I am charmed to hear it. It is a reformation.

mrs. cheveley. Yes. I can't bear so upright a gentleman, so honourable an English gentleman, being so shamefully deceived, and so—

lord goring. Well?

mrs. cheveley. I find that somehow Gertrude Chiltern's dying speech and confession has strayed into my pocket.

lord goring. What do you mean?

mrs. cheveley. [With a bitter note of triumph in her voice.] I mean that I am going to send Robert Chiltern the love-letter his wife wrote to you to-night.

lord goring. Love-letter?

mrs. cheveley. [Laughing.] 'I want you. I trust you. I am coming to you. Gertrude.'

[lord goring rushes to the bureau and takes up the envelope, finds is empty, and turns round.]

lord goring. You wretched woman, must you always be thieving? Give me back that letter. I'll take it from you by force. You shall not leave my room till I have got it.

[He *rushes towards her, but* mrs. cheveley *at once puts her hand on the electric bell that is on the table. The bell sounds with shrill reverberations, and* phipps *enters.*]

mrs. cheveley. [After a pause.] Lord Goring merely rang that you should show me out. Good-night, Lord Goring!

[*Goes out followed by* phipps. *Her face is illumined with evil triumph. There is joy in her eyes. Youth seems to have come back to her. Her last glance is like a swift arrow.* lord goring *bites his lip, and lights his a cigarette.*]

ACT DROPS

FOURTH ACT

SCENE

Same as Act II.

[lord goring *is standing by the fireplace with his hands in his pockets. He is looking rather bored.*]

lord goring. [Pulls out his watch, inspects it, and rings the bell.] It is a great nuisance. I can't find any one in this house to talk to. And I am full of interesting information. I feel like the latest edition of something or other.

[*Enter servant.*]

james. Sir Robert is still at the Foreign Office, my lord.

lord goring. Lady Chiltern not down yet?

james. Her ladyship has not yet left her room. Miss Chiltern has just come in from riding.

lord goring. [To himself.] Ah! that is something.

james. Lord Caversham has been waiting some time in the library for Sir Robert. I told him your lordship was here.

lord goring. Thank you! Would you kindly tell him I've gone?

james. [Bowing.] I shall do so, my lord.

[*Exit* servant.]

lord goring. Really, I don't want to meet my father three days running. It is a great deal too much excitement for any son. I hope to goodness he won't come up. Fathers should be neither seen nor heard. That is the only proper basis for family life. Mothers are different. Mothers are darlings. [Throws himself down into a chair, picks up a paper and begins to read it.]

[*Enter* lord caversham.]

lord caversham. Well, sir, what are you doing here? Wasting your time as usual, I suppose?

lord goring. [Throws down paper and rises.] My dear father, when one pays a visit it is for the purpose of wasting other people's time, not one's own.

lord caversham. Have you been thinking over what I spoke to you about last night?

lord goring. I have been thinking about nothing else.

lord caversham. Engaged to be married yet?

lord goring. [Genially.] Not yet: but I hope to be before lunch-time.

lord caversham. [Caustically.] You can have till dinner-time if it would be of any convenience to you.

lord goring. Thanks awfully, but I think I'd sooner be engaged before lunch.

lord caversham. Humph! Never know when you are serious or not.

lord goring. Neither do I, father.

[A pause.]

lord caversham. I suppose you have read The Times this morning?

lord goring. [Airily.] The Times? Certainly not. I only read The Morning Post. All that one should know about modern life is where the Duchesses are; anything else is quite demoralising.

lord caversham. Do you mean to say you have not read The Times leading article on Robert Chiltern's career?

lord goring. Good heavens! No. What does it say?

lord caversham. What should it say, sir? Everything complimentary, of course. Chiltern's speech last night on this Argentine Canal scheme was one of the finest pieces of oratory ever delivered in the House since Canning.

lord goring. Ah! Never heard of Canning. Never wanted to. And did

. . . did Chiltern uphold the scheme?

lord caversham. Uphold it, sir? How little you know him! Why, he denounced it roundly, and the whole system of modern political finance. This speech is the turning-point in his career, as The Times points out. You should read this article, sir. [Opens The Times.] 'Sir Robert Chiltern . . . most rising of our young statesmen . . . Brilliant orator . . . Unblemished career . . . Well-known integrity of character . . . Represents what is best in English public life . . . Noble contrast to the lax morality so common among foreign politicians.' They will never say that of you, sir.

lord goring. I sincerely hope not, father. However, I am delighted at what you tell me about Robert, thoroughly delighted. It shows he has got pluck.

lord caversham. He has got more than pluck, sir, he has got genius.

lord goring. Ah! I prefer pluck. It is not so common, nowadays, as genius is.

lord caversham. I wish you would go into Parliament.

lord goring. My dear father, only people who look dull ever get into the House of Commons, and only people who are dull ever succeed there.

lord caversham. Why don't you try to do something useful in life?

lord goring. I am far too young.

lord caversham. [Testily.] I hate this affectation of youth, sir. It is a great deal too prevalent nowadays.

lord goring. Youth isn't an affectation. Youth is an art.

lord caversham. Why don't you propose to that pretty Miss Chiltern?

lord goring. I am of a very nervous disposition, especially in the morning.

lord caversham. I don't suppose there is the smallest chance of her accepting you.

lord goring. I don't know how the betting stands to-day.

lord caversham. If she did accept you she would be the prettiest fool in England.

lord goring. That is just what I should like to marry. A thoroughly sensible wife would reduce me to a condition of absolute idiocy in less than six months.

lord caversham. You don't deserve her, sir.

lord goring. My dear father, if we men married the women we deserved, we should have a very bad time of it.

[*Enter* mabel chiltern.]

mabel chiltern. Oh! . . . How do you do, Lord Caversham? I hope Lady Caversham is quite well?

lord caversham. Lady Caversham is as usual, as usual.

lord goring. Good morning, Miss Mabel!

mabel chiltern. [Taking no notice at all of lord goring, and addressing herself exclusively to lord caversham.] And Lady Caversham's bonnets . . . are they at all better?

lord caversham. They have had a serious relapse, I am sorry to say.

lord goring. Good morning, Miss Mabel!

mabel chiltern. [To lord caversham.] I hope an operation will not be necessary.

lord caversham. [Smiling at her pertness.] If it is, we shall have to give Lady Caversham a narcotic. Otherwise she would never consent to have a feather touched.

lord goring. [With increased emphasis.] Good morning, Miss Mabel!

mabel chiltern. [Turning round with feigned surprise.] Oh, are you here? Of course you understand that after your breaking your appointment I am never going to speak to you again.

lord goring. Oh, please don't say such a thing. You are the one person in London I really like to have to listen to me.

mabel chiltern. Lord Goring, I never believe a single word that either you or I say to each other.

lord caversham. You are quite right, my dear, quite right . . . as far as he is concerned, I mean.

mabel chiltern. Do you think you could possibly make your son behave a little better occasionally? Just as a change.

lord caversham. I regret to say, Miss Chiltern, that I have no influence at all over my son. I wish I had. If I had, I know what I would make him do.

mabel chiltern. I am afraid that he has one of those terribly weak natures that are not susceptible to influence.

lord caversham. He is very heartless, very heartless.

lord goring. It seems to me that I am a little in the way here.

mabel chiltern. It is very good for you to be in the way, and to know what people say of you behind your back.

lord goring. I don't at all like knowing what people say of me behind my back. It makes me far too conceited.

lord caversham. After that, my dear, I really must bid you good morning.

mabel chiltern. Oh! I hope you are not going to leave me all alone with Lord Goring? Especially at such an early hour in the day.

lord caversham. I am afraid I can't take him with me to Downing Street. It is not the Prime Minster's day for seeing the unemployed.

[*Shakes hands with* mabel chiltern, *takes up his hat and stick, and goes out, with a parting glare of indignation at* lord goring.]

mabel chiltern. [Takes up roses and begins to arrange them in a bowl on the table.] People who don't keep their appointments in the Park are horrid.

lord goring. Detestable.

mabel chiltern. I am glad you admit it. But I wish you wouldn't look so pleased about it.

lord goring. I can't help it. I always look pleased when I am with you.

mabel chiltern. [Sadly.] Then I suppose it is my duty to remain with you?

lord goring. Of course it is.

mabel chiltern. Well, my duty is a thing I never do, on principle. It always depresses me. So I am afraid I must leave you.

lord goring. Please don't, Miss Mabel. I have something very particular to say to you.

mabel chiltern. [Rapturously.] Oh! is it a proposal?

lord goring. [Somewhat taken aback.] Well, yes, it is—I am bound to say it is.

mabel chiltern. [With a sigh of pleasure.] I am so glad. That makes the second to-day.

lord goring. [Indignantly.] The second to-day? What conceited ass has been impertinent enough to dare to propose to you before I had proposed to you?

mabel chiltern. Tommy Trafford, of course. It is one of Tommy's days for proposing. He always proposes on Tuesdays and Thursdays, during the Season.

lord goring. You didn't accept him, I hope?

mabel chiltern. I make it a rule never to accept Tommy. That is why he goes on proposing. Of course, as you didn't turn up this morning, I very nearly said yes. It would have been an excellent lesson both for him and for you if I had. It would have taught you both better manners.

lord goring. Oh! bother Tommy Trafford. Tommy is a silly little ass. I love you.

mabel chiltern. I know. And I think you might have mentioned it before. I am sure I have given you heaps of opportunities.

lord goring. Mabel, do be serious. Please be serious.

mabel chiltern. Ah! that is the sort of thing a man always says to a girl before he has been married to her. He never says it afterwards.

lord goring. [Taking hold of her hand.] Mabel, I have told you that I love you. Can't you love me a little in return?

mabel chiltern. You silly Arthur! If you knew anything about . . . anything, which you don't, you would know that I adore you. Every one in London knows it except you. It is a public scandal the way I adore you. I have been going about for the last six months telling the whole of society that I adore you. I wonder you consent to have anything to say to me. I have no character left at all. At least, I feel so happy that I am quite sure I have no character left at all.

lord goring. [Catches her in his arms and kisses her. Then there is a pause of bliss.] Dear! Do you know I was awfully afraid of being refused!

mabel chiltern. [Looking up at him.] But you never have been refused yet by anybody, have you, Arthur? I can't imagine any one refusing you.

lord goring. [After kissing her again.] Of course I'm not nearly good enough for you, Mabel.

mabel chiltern. [Nestling close to him.] I am so glad, darling. I was afraid you were.

lord goring. [After some hesitation.] And I'm . . . I'm a little over thirty.

mabel chiltern. Dear, you look weeks younger than that.

lord goring. [Enthusiastically.] How sweet of you to say so! . . . And it

106

is only fair to tell you frankly that I am fearfully extravagant.

mabel chiltern. But so am I, Arthur. So we're sure to agree. And now I must go and see Gertrude.

lord goring. Must you really? [Kisses her.]

mabel chiltern. Yes.

lord goring. Then do tell her I want to talk to her particularly. I have been waiting here all the morning to see either her or Robert.

mabel chiltern. Do you mean to say you didn't come here expressly to propose to me?

lord goring. [Triumphantly.] No; that was a flash of genius.

mabel chiltern. Your first.

lord goring. [With determination.] My last.

mabel chiltern. I am delighted to hear it. Now don't stir. I'll be back in five minutes. And don't fall into any temptations while I am away.

lord goring. Dear Mabel, while you are away, there are none. It makes me horribly dependent on you.

[Enter lady chiltern.]

lady chiltern. Good morning, dear! How pretty you are looking!

mabel chiltern. How pale you are looking, Gertrude! It is most becoming!

lady chiltern. Good morning, Lord Goring!

lord goring. [Bowing.] Good morning, Lady Chiltern!

mabel chiltern. [Aside to lord goring.] I shall be in the conservatory under the second palm tree on the left.

lord goring. Second on the left?

mabel chiltern. [With a look of mock surprise.] Yes; the usual palm tree.

[*Blows a kiss to him, unobserved by* lady chiltern, *and goes out.*]

lord goring. Lady Chiltern, I have a certain amount of very good news to tell you. Mrs. Cheveley gave me up Robert's letter last night, and I burned it. Robert is safe.

lady chiltern. [Sinking on the sofa.] Safe! Oh! I am so glad of that. What a good friend you are to him—to us!

lord goring. There is only one person now that could be said to be in any danger.

lady chiltern. Who is that?

lord goring. [Sitting down beside her.] Yourself.

lady chiltern. I? In danger? What do you mean?

lord goring. Danger is too great a word. It is a word I should not have used. But I admit I have something to tell you that may distress you, that terribly distresses me. Yesterday evening you wrote me a very beautiful, womanly letter, asking me for my help. You wrote to me as one of your oldest friends, one of your husband's oldest friends. Mrs. Cheveley stole that letter from my rooms.

lady chiltern. Well, what use is it to her? Why should she not have it?

lord goring. [Rising.] Lady Chiltern, I will be quite frank with you. Mrs. Cheveley puts a certain construction on that letter and proposes to send it to your husband.

lady chiltern. But what construction could she put on it? . . . Oh! not that! not that! If I in—in trouble, and wanting your help, trusting you, propose to come to you . . . that you may advise me . . . assist me . . . Oh! are there women so horrible as that . . .? And she proposes to send it to my husband? Tell me what happened. Tell me all that happened.

lord goring. Mrs. Cheveley was concealed in a room adjoining my library, without my knowledge. I thought that the person who was waiting in that room to see me was yourself. Robert came in unexpectedly. A chair or something fell in the room. He forced his way in, and he discovered her. We had a terrible scene. I still thought it was you. He left me in anger. At the end of everything Mrs. Cheveley got possession of your letter—she stole it, when or how, I don't know.

lady chiltern. At what hour did this happen?

lord goring. At half-past ten. And now I propose that we tell Robert the whole thing at once.

lady chiltern. [Looking at him with amazement that is almost terror.] You want me to tell Robert that the woman you expected was not Mrs. Cheveley, but myself? That it was I whom you thought was concealed in a room in your house, at half-past ten o'clock at night? You want me to tell him that?

lord goring. I think it is better that he should know the exact truth.

lady chiltern. [Rising.] Oh, I couldn't, I couldn't!

lord goring. May I do it?

lady chiltern. No.

lord goring. [Gravely.] You are wrong, Lady Chiltern.

lady chiltern. No. The letter must be intercepted. That is all. But how can I do it? Letters arrive for him every moment of the day. His secretaries open them and hand them to him. I dare not ask the servants to bring me his letters. It would be impossible. Oh! why don't you tell me what to do?

lord goring. Pray be calm, Lady Chiltern, and answer the questions I am going to put to you. You said his secretaries open his letters.

lady chiltern. Yes.

lord goring. Who is with him to-day? Mr. Trafford, isn't it?

lady chiltern. No. Mr. Montford, I think.

lord goring. You can trust him?

lady chiltern. [With a gesture of despair.] Oh! how do I know?

lord goring. He would do what you asked him, wouldn't he?

lady chiltern. I think so.

lord goring. Your letter was on pink paper. He could recognise it without reading it, couldn't he? By the colour?

lady chiltern. I suppose so.

lord goring. Is he in the house now?

lady chiltern. Yes.

lord goring. Then I will go and see him myself, and tell him that a certain letter, written on pink paper, is to be forwarded to Robert to-day, and that at all costs it must not reach him. [Goes to the door, and opens it.] Oh! Robert is coming upstairs with the letter in his hand. It has reached him already.

lady chiltern. [With a cry of pain.] Oh! you have saved his life; what have you done with mine?

[*Enter* sir robert chiltern. *He has the letter in his hand, and is reading it. He comes towards his wife, not noticing lord goring's presence.*]

sir robert chiltern. 'I want you. I trust you. I am coming to you. Gertrude.' Oh, my love! Is this true? Do you indeed trust me, and want me? If so, it was for me to come to you, not for you to write of coming to me. This letter of yours, Gertrude, makes me feel that nothing that the world may do can hurt me now. You want me, Gertrude?

[lord goring, *unseen by* sir robert chiltern, *makes an imploring sign to* lady chiltern *to accept the situation and* sir robert's *error.*]

lady chiltern. Yes.

sir robert chiltern. You trust me, Gertrude?

lady chiltern. Yes.

sir robert chiltern. Ah! why did you not add you loved me?

lady chiltern. [Taking his hand.] Because I loved you.

[lord goring *passes into the conservatory*.]

sir robert chiltern. [Kisses her.] Gertrude, you don't know what I feel. When Montford passed me your letter across the table—he had opened it by mistake, I suppose, without looking at the handwriting on the envelope— and I read it—oh! I did not care what disgrace or punishment was in store for me, I only thought you loved me still.

lady chiltern. There is no disgrace in store for you, nor any public shame. Mrs. Cheveley has handed over to Lord Goring the document that was in her possession, and he has destroyed it.

sir robert chiltern. Are you sure of this, Gertrude?

lady chiltern. Yes; Lord Goring has just told me.

sir robert chiltern. Then I am safe! Oh! what a wonderful thing to be safe! For two days I have been in terror. I am safe now. How did Arthur destroy my letter? Tell me.

lady chiltern. He burned it.

sir robert chiltern. I wish I had seen that one sin of my youth burning to ashes. How many men there are in modern life who would like to see their past burning to white ashes before them! Is Arthur still here?

lady chiltern. Yes; he is in the conservatory.

sir robert chiltern. I am so glad now I made that speech last night in the House, so glad. I made it thinking that public disgrace might be the result. But it has not been so.

lady chiltern. Public honour has been the result.

sir robert chiltern. I think so. I fear so, almost. For although I am safe from detection, although every proof against me is destroyed, I suppose, Gertrude . . . I suppose I should retire from public life? [He looks anxiously at his wife.]

lady chiltern. [Eagerly.] Oh yes, Robert, you should do that. It is your duty to do that.

sir robert chiltern. It is much to surrender.

lady chiltern. No; it will be much to gain.

[sir robert chiltern *walks up and down the room with a troubled expression. Then comes over to his wife, and puts his hand on her shoulder.*]

sir robert chiltern. And you would be happy living somewhere alone with me, abroad perhaps, or in the country away from London, away from public life? You would have no regrets?

lady chiltern. Oh! none, Robert.

sir robert chiltern. [Sadly.] And your ambition for me? You used to be ambitious for me.

lady chiltern. Oh, my ambition! I have none now, but that we two may love each other. It was your ambition that led you astray. Let us not talk about ambition.

[lord goring *returns from the conservatory, looking very pleased with himself, and with an entirely new buttonhole that some one has made for him.*]

sir robert chiltern. [Going towards him.] Arthur, I have to thank you for what you have done for me. I don't know how I can repay you. [Shakes hands with him.]

lord goring. My dear fellow, I'll tell you at once. At the present moment, under the usual palm tree . . . I mean in the conservatory . . .

[*Enter* mason.]

mason. Lord Caversham.

lord goring. That admirable father of mine really makes a habit of

112

turning up at the wrong moment. It is very heartless of him, very heartless indeed.

[*Enter* lord caversham. mason *goes out.*]

lord caversham. Good morning, Lady Chiltern! Warmest congratulations to you, Chiltern, on your brilliant speech last night. I have just left the Prime Minister, and you are to have the vacant seat in the Cabinet.

sir robert chiltern. [With a look of joy and triumph.] A seat in the Cabinet?

lord caversham. Yes; here is the Prime Minister's letter. [Hands letter.]

sir robert chiltern. [Takes letter and reads it.] A seat in the Cabinet!

lord caversham. Certainly, and you well deserve it too. You have got what we want so much in political life nowadays—high character, high moral tone, high principles. [To lord goring.] Everything that you have not got, sir, and never will have.

lord goring. I don't like principles, father. I prefer prejudices.

[sir robert chiltern *is on the brink of accepting the Prime Minister's offer, when he sees wife looking at him with her clear, candid eyes. He then realises that it is impossible.*]

sir robert chiltern. I cannot accept this offer, Lord Caversham. I have made up my mind to decline it.

lord caversham. Decline it, sir!

sir robert chiltern. My intention is to retire at once from public life.

lord caversham. [Angrily.] Decline a seat in the Cabinet, and retire from public life? Never heard such damned nonsense in the whole course of my existence. I beg your pardon, Lady Chiltern. Chiltern, I beg your pardon. [To lord goring.] Don't grin like that, sir.

lord goring. No, father.

lord caversham. Lady Chiltern, you are a sensible woman, the most sensible woman in London, the most sensible woman I know. Will you kindly prevent your husband from making such a . . . from taking such . . . Will you kindly do that, Lady Chiltern?

lady chiltern. I think my husband in right in his determination, Lord Caversham. I approve of it.

lord caversham. You approve of it? Good heavens!

lady chiltern. [Taking her husband's hand.] I admire him for it. I admire him immensely for it. I have never admired him so much before. He is finer than even I thought him. [To sir robert chiltern.] You will go and write your letter to the Prime Minister now, won't you? Don't hesitate about it, Robert.

sir robert chiltern. [With a touch of bitterness.] I suppose I had better write it at once. Such offers are not repeated. I will ask you to excuse me for a moment, Lord Caversham.

lady chiltern. I may come with you, Robert, may I not?

sir robert chiltern. Yes, Gertrude.

[lady chiltern *goes out with him.*]

lord caversham. What is the matter with this family? Something wrong here, eh? [Tapping his forehead.] Idiocy? Hereditary, I suppose. Both of them, too. Wife as well as husband. Very sad. Very sad indeed! And they are not an old family. Can't understand it.

lord goring. It is not idiocy, father, I assure you.

lord caversham. What is it then, sir?

lord goring. [After some hesitation.] Well, it is what is called nowadays a high moral tone, father. That is all.

lord caversham. Hate these new-fangled names. Same thing as we used to call idiocy fifty years ago. Shan't stay in this house any longer.

lord goring. [Taking his arm.] Oh! just go in here for a moment, father.

114

Third palm tree to the left, the usual palm tree.

lord caversham. What, sir?

lord goring. I beg your pardon, father, I forgot. The conservatory, father, the conservatory—there is some one there I want you to talk to.

lord caversham. What about, sir?

lord goring. About me, father,

lord caversham. [Grimly.] Not a subject on which much eloquence is possible.

lord goring. No, father; but the lady is like me. She doesn't care much for eloquence in others. She thinks it a little loud.

[lord caversham goes out into the conservatory. lady chiltern enters.]

lord goring. Lady Chiltern, why are you playing Mrs. Cheveley's cards?

lady chiltern. [Startled.] I don't understand you.

lord goring. Mrs. Cheveley made an attempt to ruin your husband. Either to drive him from public life, or to make him adopt a dishonourable position. From the latter tragedy you saved him. The former you are now thrusting on him. Why should you do him the wrong Mrs. Cheveley tried to do and failed?

lady chiltern. Lord Goring?

lord goring. [Pulling himself together for a great effort, and showing the philosopher that underlies the dandy.] Lady Chiltern, allow me. You wrote me a letter last night in which you said you trusted me and wanted my help. Now is the moment when you really want my help, now is the time when you have got to trust me, to trust in my counsel and judgment. You love Robert. Do you want to kill his love for you? What sort of existence will he have if you rob him of the fruits of his ambition, if you take him from the splendour of a great political career, if you close the doors of public life against him, if you condemn him to sterile failure, he who was made for

115

triumph and success? Women are not meant to judge us, but to forgive us when we need forgiveness. Pardon, not punishment, is their mission. Why should you scourge him with rods for a sin done in his youth, before he knew you, before he knew himself? A man's life is of more value than a woman's. It has larger issues, wider scope, greater ambitions. A woman's life revolves in curves of emotions. It is upon lines of intellect that a man's life progresses. Don't make any terrible mistake, Lady Chiltern. A woman who can keep a man's love, and love him in return, has done all the world wants of women, or should want of them.

lady chiltern. [Troubled and hesitating.] But it is my husband himself who wishes to retire from public life. He feels it is his duty. It was he who first said so.

lord goring. Rather than lose your love, Robert would do anything, wreck his whole career, as he is on the brink of doing now. He is making for you a terrible sacrifice. Take my advice, Lady Chiltern, and do not accept a sacrifice so great. If you do, you will live to repent it bitterly. We men and women are not made to accept such sacrifices from each other. We are not worthy of them. Besides, Robert has been punished enough.

lady chiltern. We have both been punished. I set him up too high.

lord goring. [With deep feeling in his voice.] Do not for that reason set him down now too low. If he has fallen from his altar, do not thrust him into the mire. Failure to Robert would be the very mire of shame. Power is his passion. He would lose everything, even his power to feel love. Your husband's life is at this moment in your hands, your husband's love is in your hands. Don't mar both for him.

[*Enter* sir robert chiltern.]

sir robert chiltern. Gertrude, here is the draft of my letter. Shall I read it to you?

lady chiltern. Let me see it.

[sir robert *hands her the letter. She reads it, and then, with a gesture of*

116

passion, tears it up.]

sir robert chiltern. What are you doing?

lady chiltern. A man's life is of more value than a woman's. It has larger issues, wider scope, greater ambitions. Our lives revolve in curves of emotions. It is upon lines of intellect that a man's life progresses. I have just learnt this, and much else with it, from Lord Goring. And I will not spoil your life for you, nor see you spoil it as a sacrifice to me, a useless sacrifice!

sir robert chiltern. Gertrude! Gertrude!

lady chiltern. You can forget. Men easily forget. And I forgive. That is how women help the world. I see that now.

sir robert chiltern. [Deeply overcome by emotion, embraces her.] My wife! my wife! [To lord goring.] Arthur, it seems that I am always to be in your debt.

lord goring. Oh dear no, Robert. Your debt is to Lady Chiltern, not to me!

sir robert chiltern. I owe you much. And now tell me what you were going to ask me just now as Lord Caversham came in.

lord goring. Robert, you are your sister's guardian, and I want your consent to my marriage with her. That is all.

lady chiltern. Oh, I am so glad! I am so glad! [Shakes hands with lord goring.]

lord goring. Thank you, Lady Chiltern.

sir robert chiltern. [With a troubled look.] My sister to be your wife?

lord goring. Yes.

sir robert chiltern. [Speaking with great firmness.] Arthur, I am very sorry, but the thing is quite out of the question. I have to think of Mabel's future happiness. And I don't think her happiness would be safe in your hands. And I cannot have her sacrificed!

lord goring. Sacrificed!

sir robert chiltern. Yes, utterly sacrificed. Loveless marriages are horrible. But there is one thing worse than an absolutely loveless marriage. A marriage in which there is love, but on one side only; faith, but on one side only; devotion, but on one side only, and in which of the two hearts one is sure to be broken.

lord goring. But I love Mabel. No other woman has any place in my life.

lady chiltern. Robert, if they love each other, why should they not be married?

sir robert chiltern. Arthur cannot bring Mabel the love that she deserves.

lord goring. What reason have you for saying that?

sir robert chiltern. [After a pause.] Do you really require me to tell you?

lord goring. Certainly I do.

sir robert chiltern. As you choose. When I called on you yesterday evening I found Mrs. Cheveley concealed in your rooms. It was between ten and eleven o'clock at night. I do not wish to say anything more. Your relations with Mrs. Cheveley have, as I said to you last night, nothing whatsoever to do with me. I know you were engaged to be married to her once. The fascination she exercised over you then seems to have returned. You spoke to me last night of her as of a woman pure and stainless, a woman whom you respected and honoured. That may be so. But I cannot give my sister's life into your hands. It would be wrong of me. It would be unjust, infamously unjust to her.

lord goring. I have nothing more to say.

lady chiltern. Robert, it was not Mrs. Cheveley whom Lord Goring expected last night.

sir robert chiltern. Not Mrs. Cheveley! Who was it then?

lord goring. Lady Chiltern!

lady chiltern. It was your own wife. Robert, yesterday afternoon Lord Goring told me that if ever I was in trouble I could come to him for help, as he was our oldest and best friend. Later on, after that terrible scene in this room, I wrote to him telling him that I trusted him, that I had need of him, that I was coming to him for help and advice. [sir robert chiltern takes the letter out of his pocket.] Yes, that letter. I didn't go to Lord Goring's, after all. I felt that it is from ourselves alone that help can come. Pride made me think that. Mrs. Cheveley went. She stole my letter and sent it anonymously to you this morning, that you should think . . . Oh! Robert, I cannot tell you what she wished you to think. . . .

sir robert chiltern. What! Had I fallen so low in your eyes that you thought that even for a moment I could have doubted your goodness? Gertrude, Gertrude, you are to me the white image of all good things, and sin can never touch you. Arthur, you can go to Mabel, and you have my best wishes! Oh! stop a moment. There is no name at the beginning of this letter. The brilliant Mrs. Cheveley does not seem to have noticed that. There should be a name.

lady chiltern. Let me write yours. It is you I trust and need. You and none else.

lord goring. Well, really, Lady Chiltern, I think I should have back my own letter.

lady chiltern. [Smiling.] No; you shall have Mabel. [Takes the letter and writes her husband's name on it.]

lord goring. Well, I hope she hasn't changed her mind. It's nearly twenty minutes since I saw her last.

[Enter mabel chiltern and lord caversham.]

mabel chiltern. Lord Goring, I think your father's conversation much more improving than yours. I am only going to talk to Lord Caversham in the future, and always under the usual palm tree.

lord goring. Darling! [Kisses her.]

lord caversham. [Considerably taken aback.] What does this mean, sir? You don't mean to say that this charming, clever young lady has been so foolish as to accept you?

lord goring. Certainly, father! And Chiltern's been wise enough to accept the seat in the Cabinet.

lord caversham. I am very glad to hear that, Chiltern . . . I congratulate you, sir. If the country doesn't go to the dogs or the Radicals, we shall have you Prime Minister, some day.

[*Enter* mason.]

mason. Luncheon is on the table, my Lady!

[mason *goes out.*]

mabel chiltern. You'll stop to luncheon, Lord Caversham, won't you?

lord caversham. With pleasure, and I'll drive you down to Downing Street afterwards, Chiltern. You have a great future before you, a great future. Wish I could say the same for you, sir. [To lord goring.] But your career will have to be entirely domestic.

lord goring. Yes, father, I prefer it domestic.

lord caversham. And if you don't make this young lady an ideal husband, I'll cut you off with a shilling.

mabel chiltern. An ideal husband! Oh, I don't think I should like that. It sounds like something in the next world.

lord caversham. What do you want him to be then, dear?

mabel chiltern. He can be what he chooses. All I want is to be . . . to be . . . oh! a real wife to him.

lord caversham. Upon my word, there is a good deal of common sense in that, Lady Chiltern.

[*They all go out except* sir robert chiltern. *He sinks in a chair, wrapt in*

120

thought. After a little time lady chiltern *returns to look for him.*]

lady chiltern. [Leaning over the back of the chair.] Aren't you coming in, Robert?

sir robert chiltern. [Taking her hand.] Gertrude, is it love you feel for me, or is it pity merely?

lady chiltern. [Kisses him.] It is love, Robert. Love, and only love. For both of us a new life is beginning.

CURTAIN

CHARMIDES AND OTHER POEMS

CHARMIDES

I.

He was a Grecian lad, who coming home
   With pulpy figs and wine from Sicily
Stood at his galley's prow, and let the foam
   Blow through his crisp brown curls unconsciously,
And holding wave and wind in boy's despite
Peered from his dripping seat across the wet and stormy night.

Till with the dawn he saw a burnished spear
   Like a thin thread of gold against the sky,
And hoisted sail, and strained the creaking gear,
   And bade the pilot head her lustily
Against the nor'west gale, and all day long
Held on his way, and marked the rowers' time with measured song.

And when the faint Corinthian hills were red
   Dropped anchor in a little sandy bay,
And with fresh boughs of olive crowned his head,
   And brushed from cheek and throat the hoary spray,
And washed his limbs with oil, and from the hold

Brought out his linen tunic and his sandals brazen-soled,

And a rich robe stained with the fishers' juice
  Which of some swarthy trader he had bought
Upon the sunny quay at Syracuse,
  And was with Tyrian broideries inwrought,
And by the questioning merchants made his way
Up through the soft and silver woods, and when the labouring day

Had spun its tangled web of crimson cloud,
  Clomb the high hill, and with swift silent feet
Crept to the fane unnoticed by the crowd
  Of busy priests, and from some dark retreat
Watched the young swains his frolic playmates bring
The firstling of their little flock, and the shy shepherd fling

The crackling salt upon the flame, or hang
  His studded crook against the temple wall
To Her who keeps away the ravenous fang
  Of the base wolf from homestead and from stall;
And then the clear-voiced maidens 'gan to sing,
And to the altar each man brought some goodly offering,

A beechen cup brimming with milky foam,

A fair cloth wrought with cunning imagery

Of hounds in chase, a waxen honey-comb

   Dripping with oozy gold which scarce the bee

Had ceased from building, a black skin of oil

Meet for the wrestlers, a great boar the fierce and white-tusked spoil

Stolen from Artemis that jealous maid

   To please Athena, and the dappled hide

Of a tall stag who in some mountain glade

   Had met the shaft; and then the herald cried,

And from the pillared precinct one by one

Went the glad Greeks well pleased that they their simple vows had done.

And the old priest put out the waning fires

   Save that one lamp whose restless ruby glowed

For ever in the cell, and the shrill lyres

   Came fainter on the wind, as down the road

In joyous dance these country folk did pass,

And with stout hands the warder closed the gates of polished brass.

Long time he lay and hardly dared to breathe,

   And heard the cadenced drip of spilt-out wine,

And the rose-petals falling from the wreath

As the night breezes wandered through the shrine,

And seemed to be in some entrancèd swoon

Till through the open roof above the full and brimming moon

Flooded with sheeny waves the marble floor,

   When from his nook up leapt the venturous lad,

And flinging wide the cedar-carven door

   Beheld an awful image saffron-clad

And armed for battle! the gaunt Griffin glared

From the huge helm, and the long lance of wreck and ruin flared

Like a red rod of flame, stony and steeled

   The Gorgon's head its leaden eyeballs rolled,

And writhed its snaky horrors through the shield,

   And gaped aghast with bloodless lips and cold

In passion impotent, while with blind gaze

The blinking owl between the feet hooted in shrill amaze.

The lonely fisher as he trimmed his lamp

   Far out at sea off Sunium, or cast

The net for tunnies, heard a brazen tramp

   Of horses smite the waves, and a wild blast

Divide the folded curtains of the night,

And knelt upon the little poop, and prayed in holy fright.

And guilty lovers in their venery
  Forgat a little while their stolen sweets,
Deeming they heard dread Dian's bitter cry;
  And the grim watchmen on their lofty seats
Ran to their shields in haste precipitate,
Or strained black-bearded throats across the dusky parapet.

For round the temple rolled the clang of arms,
  And the twelve Gods leapt up in marble fear,
And the air quaked with dissonant alarums
  Till huge Poseidon shook his mighty spear,
And on the frieze the prancing horses neighed,
And the low tread of hurrying feet rang from the cavalcade.

Ready for death with parted lips he stood,
  And well content at such a price to see
That calm wide brow, that terrible maidenhood,
  The marvel of that pitiless chastity,
Ah! well content indeed, for never wight
Since Troy's young shepherd prince had seen so wonderful a sight.

Ready for death he stood, but lo! the air

Grew silent, and the horses ceased to neigh,

And off his brow he tossed the clustering hair,

And from his limbs he throw the cloak away;

For whom would not such love make desperate?

And nigher came, and touched her throat, and with hands violate

Undid the cuirass, and the crocus gown,

And bared the breasts of polished ivory,

Till from the waist the peplos falling down

Left visible the secret mystery

Which to no lover will Athena show,

The grand cool flanks, the crescent thighs, the bossy hills of snow.

Those who have never known a lover's sin

Let them not read my ditty, it will be

To their dull ears so musicless and thin

That they will have no joy of it, but ye

To whose wan cheeks now creeps the lingering smile,

Ye who have learned who Eros is,—O listen yet awhile.

A little space he let his greedy eyes

Rest on the burnished image, till mere sight

Half swooned for surfeit of such luxuries,

And then his lips in hungering delight

Fed on her lips, and round the towered neck

He flung his arms, nor cared at all his passion's will to check.

Never I ween did lover hold such tryst,

  For all night long he murmured honeyed word,

And saw her sweet unravished limbs, and kissed

  Her pale and argent body undisturbed,

And paddled with the polished throat, and pressed

His hot and beating heart upon her chill and icy breast.

It was as if Numidian javelins

  Pierced through and through his wild and whirling brain,

And his nerves thrilled like throbbing violins

  In exquisite pulsation, and the pain

Was such sweet anguish that he never drew

His lips from hers till overhead the lark of warning flew.

They who have never seen the daylight peer

  Into a darkened room, and drawn the curtain,

And with dull eyes and wearied from some dear

  And worshipped body risen, they for certain

Will never know of what I try to sing,

How long the last kiss was, how fond and late his lingering.

The moon was girdled with a crystal rim,
  The sign which shipmen say is ominous
Of wrath in heaven, the wan stars were dim,
  And the low lightening east was tremulous
With the faint fluttering wings of flying dawn,
Ere from the silent sombre shrine his lover had withdrawn.

Down the steep rock with hurried feet and fast
  Clomb the brave lad, and reached the cave of Pan,
And heard the goat-foot snoring as he passed,
  And leapt upon a grassy knoll and ran
Like a young fawn unto an olive wood
Which in a shady valley by the well-built city stood;

And sought a little stream, which well he knew,
  For oftentimes with boyish careless shout
The green and crested grebe he would pursue,
  Or snare in woven net the silver trout,
And down amid the startled reeds he lay
Panting in breathless sweet affright, and waited for the day.

On the green bank he lay, and let one hand

Dip in the cool dark eddies listlessly,

And soon the breath of morning came and fanned

His hot flushed cheeks, or lifted wantonly

The tangled curls from off his forehead, while

He on the running water gazed with strange and secret smile.

And soon the shepherd in rough woollen cloak

With his long crook undid the wattled cotes,

And from the stack a thin blue wreath of smoke

Curled through the air across the ripening oats,

And on the hill the yellow house-dog bayed

As through the crisp and rustling fern the heavy cattle strayed.

And when the light-foot mower went afield

Across the meadows laced with threaded dew,

And the sheep bleated on the misty weald,

And from its nest the waking corncrake flew,

Some woodmen saw him lying by the stream

And marvelled much that any lad so beautiful could seem,

Nor deemed him born of mortals, and one said,

'It is young Hylas, that false runaway

Who with a Naiad now would make his bed

Forgetting Herakles,' but others, 'Nay,

It is Narcissus, his own paramour,

Those are the fond and crimson lips no woman can allure.'

And when they nearer came a third one cried,

  'It is young Dionysos who has hid

His spear and fawnskin by the river side

  Weary of hunting with the Bassarid,

And wise indeed were we away to fly:

They live not long who on the gods immortal come to spy.'

So turned they back, and feared to look behind,

  And told the timid swain how they had seen

Amid the reeds some woodland god reclined,

  And no man dared to cross the open green,

And on that day no olive-tree was slain,

Nor rushes cut, but all deserted was the fair domain,

Save when the neat-herd's lad, his empty pail

  Well slung upon his back, with leap and bound

Raced on the other side, and stopped to hail,

  Hoping that he some comrade new had found,

And gat no answer, and then half afraid

Passed on his simple way, or down the still and silent glade

A little girl ran laughing from the farm,
  Not thinking of love's secret mysteries,
And when she saw the white and gleaming arm
  And all his manlihood, with longing eyes
Whose passion mocked her sweet virginity
Watched him awhile, and then stole back sadly and wearily.

Far off he heard the city's hum and noise,
  And now and then the shriller laughter where
The passionate purity of brown-limbed boys
  Wrestled or raced in the clear healthful air,
And now and then a little tinkling bell
As the shorn wether led the sheep down to the mossy well.

Through the grey willows danced the fretful gnat,
  The grasshopper chirped idly from the tree,
In sleek and oily coat the water-rat
  Breasting the little ripples manfully
Made for the wild-duck's nest, from bough to bough
Hopped the shy finch, and the huge tortoise crept across the slough.

On the faint wind floated the silky seeds

As the bright scythe swept through the waving grass,

    The ouzel-cock splashed circles in the reeds

And flecked with silver whorls the forest's glass,

Which scarce had caught again its imagery

Ere from its bed the dusky tench leapt at the dragon-fly.

But little care had he for any thing

    Though up and down the beech the squirrel played,

And from the copse the linnet 'gan to sing

    To its brown mate its sweetest serenade;

Ah! little care indeed, for he had seen

The breasts of Pallas and the naked wonder of the Queen.

But when the herdsman called his straggling goats

    With whistling pipe across the rocky road,

And the shard-beetle with its trumpet-notes

    Boomed through the darkening woods, and seemed to bode

Of coming storm, and the belated crane

Passed homeward like a shadow, and the dull big drops of rain

Fell on the pattering fig-leaves, up he rose,

    And from the gloomy forest went his way

Past sombre homestead and wet orchard-close,

And came at last unto a little quay,

And called his mates aboard, and took his seat

On the high poop, and pushed from land, and loosed the dripping sheet,

And steered across the bay, and when nine suns

   Passed down the long and laddered way of gold,

And nine pale moons had breathed their orisons

   To the chaste stars their confessors, or told

Their dearest secret to the downy moth

That will not fly at noonday, through the foam and surging froth

Came a great owl with yellow sulphurous eyes

   And lit upon the ship, whose timbers creaked

As though the lading of three argosies

   Were in the hold, and flapped its wings and shrieked,

And darkness straightway stole across the deep,

Sheathed was Orion's sword, dread Mars himself fled down the steep,

And the moon hid behind a tawny mask

   Of drifting cloud, and from the ocean's marge

Rose the red plume, the huge and hornèd casque,

   The seven-cubit spear, the brazen targe!

And clad in bright and burnished panoply

Athena strode across the stretch of sick and shivering sea!

To the dull sailors' sight her loosened looks
   Seemed like the jagged storm-rack, and her feet
Only the spume that floats on hidden rocks,
   And, marking how the rising waters beat
Against the rolling ship, the pilot cried
To the young helmsman at the stern to luff to windward side

But he, the overbold adulterer,
   A dear profaner of great mysteries,
An ardent amorous idolater,
   When he beheld those grand relentless eyes
Laughed loud for joy, and crying out 'I come'
Leapt from the lofty poop into the chill and churning foam.

Then fell from the high heaven one bright star,
   One dancer left the circling galaxy,
And back to Athens on her clattering car
   In all the pride of venged divinity
Pale Pallas swept with shrill and steely clank,
And a few gurgling bubbles rose where her boy lover sank.

And the mast shuddered as the gaunt owl flew

With mocking hoots after the wrathful Queen,

And the old pilot bade the trembling crew

   Hoist the big sail, and told how he had seen

Close to the stern a dim and giant form,

And like a dipping swallow the stout ship dashed through the storm.

And no man dared to speak of Charmides

   Deeming that he some evil thing had wrought,

And when they reached the strait Symplegades

   They beached their galley on the shore, and sought

The toll-gate of the city hastily,

And in the market showed their brown and pictured pottery.

II.

But some good Triton-god had ruth, and bare

   The boy's drowned body back to Grecian land,

And mermaids combed his dank and dripping hair

   And smoothed his brow, and loosed his clenching hand;

Some brought sweet spices from far Araby,

And others bade the halcyon sing her softest lullaby.

And when he neared his old Athenian home,

   A mighty billow rose up suddenly

Upon whose oily back the clotted foam

    Lay diapered in some strange fantasy,

And clasping him unto its glassy breast

Swept landward, like a white-maned steed upon a venturous quest!

Now where Colonos leans unto the sea

    There lies a long and level stretch of lawn;

The rabbit knows it, and the mountain bee

    For it deserts Hymettus, and the Faun

Is not afraid, for never through the day

Comes a cry ruder than the shout of shepherd lads at play.

But often from the thorny labyrinth

    And tangled branches of the circling wood

The stealthy hunter sees young Hyacinth

    Hurling the polished disk, and draws his hood

Over his guilty gaze, and creeps away,

Nor dares to wind his horn, or—else at the first break of day

The Dryads come and throw the leathern ball

    Along the reedy shore, and circumvent

Some goat-eared Pan to be their seneschal

    For fear of bold Poseidon's ravishment,

And loose their girdles, with shy timorous eyes,

Lest from the surf his azure arms and purple beard should rise.

On this side and on that a rocky cave,

 Hung with the yellow-belled laburnum, stands

Smooth is the beach, save where some ebbing wave

 Leaves its faint outline etched upon the sands,

As though it feared to be too soon forgot

By the green rush, its playfellow,—and yet, it is a spot

So small, that the inconstant butterfly

 Could steal the hoarded money from each flower

Ere it was noon, and still not satisfy

 Its over-greedy love,—within an hour

A sailor boy, were he but rude enow

To land and pluck a garland for his galley's painted prow,

Would almost leave the little meadow bare,

 For it knows nothing of great pageantry,

Only a few narcissi here and there

 Stand separate in sweet austerity,

Dotting the unmown grass with silver stars,

And here and there a daffodil waves tiny scimitars.

Hither the billow brought him, and was glad
 Of such dear servitude, and where the land
Was virgin of all waters laid the lad
 Upon the golden margent of the strand,
And like a lingering lover oft returned
To kiss those pallid limbs which once with intense fire burned,

Ere the wet seas had quenched that holocaust,
 That self-fed flame, that passionate lustihead,
Ere grisly death with chill and nipping frost
 Had withered up those lilies white and red
Which, while the boy would through the forest range,
Answered each other in a sweet antiphonal counter-change.

And when at dawn the wood-nymphs, hand-in-hand,
 Threaded the bosky dell, their satyr spied
The boy's pale body stretched upon the sand,
 And feared Poseidon's treachery, and cried,
And like bright sunbeams flitting through a glade
Each startled Dryad sought some safe and leafy ambuscade.

Save one white girl, who deemed it would not be

So dread a thing to feel a sea-god's arms

Crushing her breasts in amorous tyranny,

    And longed to listen to those subtle charms

Insidious lovers weave when they would win

Some fencèd fortress, and stole back again, nor thought it sin

To yield her treasure unto one so fair,

    And lay beside him, thirsty with love's drouth,

Called him soft names, played with his tangled hair,

    And with hot lips made havoc of his mouth

Afraid he might not wake, and then afraid

Lest he might wake too soon, fled back, and then, fond renegade,

Returned to fresh assault, and all day long

    Sat at his side, and laughed at her new toy,

And held his hand, and sang her sweetest song,

    Then frowned to see how froward was the boy

Who would not with her maidenhood entwine,

Nor knew that three days since his eyes had looked on Proserpine;

Nor knew what sacrilege his lips had done,

    But said, 'He will awake, I know him well,

He will awake at evening when the sun

143

Hangs his red shield on Corinth's citadel;

This sleep is but a cruel treachery

To make me love him more, and in some cavern of the sea

Deeper than ever falls the fisher's line

   Already a huge Triton blows his horn,

And weaves a garland from the crystalline

   And drifting ocean-tendrils to adorn

The emerald pillars of our bridal bed,

For sphered in foaming silver, and with coral crownèd head,

We two will sit upon a throne of pearl,

   And a blue wave will be our canopy,

And at our feet the water-snakes will curl

   In all their amethystine panoply

Of diamonded mail, and we will mark

The mullets swimming by the mast of some storm-foundered bark,

Vermilion-finned with eyes of bossy gold

   Like flakes of crimson light, and the great deep

His glassy-portaled chamber will unfold,

   And we will see the painted dolphins sleep

Cradled by murmuring halcyons on the rocks

Where Proteus in quaint suit of green pastures his monstrous flocks.

And tremulous opal-hued anemones
   Will wave their purple fringes where we tread
Upon the mirrored floor, and argosies
   Of fishes flecked with tawny scales will thread
The drifting cordage of the shattered wreck,
And honey-coloured amber beads our twining limbs will deck.'

But when that baffled Lord of War the Sun
   With gaudy pennon flying passed away
Into his brazen House, and one by one
   The little yellow stars began to stray
Across the field of heaven, ah! then indeed
She feared his lips upon her lips would never care to feed,

And cried, 'Awake, already the pale moon
   Washes the trees with silver, and the wave
Creeps grey and chilly up this sandy dune,
   The croaking frogs are out, and from the cave
The nightjar shrieks, the fluttering bats repass,
And the brown stoat with hollow flanks creeps through the dusky grass.

Nay, though thou art a god, be not so coy,

For in yon stream there is a little reed

That often whispers how a lovely boy

   Lay with her once upon a grassy mead,

Who when his cruel pleasure he had done

Spread wings of rustling gold and soared aloft into the sun.

Be not so coy, the laurel trembles still

   With great Apollo's kisses, and the fir

Whose clustering sisters fringe the seaward hill

   Hath many a tale of that bold ravisher

Whom men call Boreas, and I have seen

The mocking eyes of Hermes through the poplar's silvery sheen.

Even the jealous Naiads call me fair,

   And every morn a young and ruddy swain

Woos me with apples and with locks of hair,

   And seeks to soothe my virginal disdain

By all the gifts the gentle wood-nymphs love;

But yesterday he brought to me an iris-plumaged dove

With little crimson feet, which with its store

   Of seven spotted eggs the cruel lad

Had stolen from the lofty sycamore

At daybreak, when her amorous comrade had

Flown off in search of berried juniper

Which most they love; the fretful wasp, that earliest vintager

Of the blue grapes, hath not persistency

  So constant as this simple shepherd-boy

For my poor lips, his joyous purity

  And laughing sunny eyes might well decoy

A Dryad from her oath to Artemis;

For very beautiful is he, his mouth was made to kiss;

His argent forehead, like a rising moon

  Over the dusky hills of meeting brows,

Is crescent shaped, the hot and Tyrian noon

  Leads from the myrtle-grove no goodlier spouse

For Cytheræa, the first silky down

Fringes his blushing cheeks, and his young limbs are strong and brown;

And he is rich, and fat and fleecy herds

  Of bleating sheep upon his meadows lie,

And many an earthen bowl of yellow curds

  Is in his homestead for the thievish fly

To swim and drown in, the pink clover mead

Keeps its sweet store for him, and he can pipe on oaten reed.

And yet I love him not; it was for thee
    I kept my love; I knew that thou would'st come
To rid me of this pallid chastity,
    Thou fairest flower of the flowerless foam
Of all the wide Ægean, brightest star
Of ocean's azure heavens where the mirrored planets are!

I knew that thou would'st come, for when at first
    The dry wood burgeoned, and the sap of spring
Swelled in my green and tender bark or burst
    To myriad multitudinous blossoming
Which mocked the midnight with its mimic moons
That did not dread the dawn, and first the thrushes' rapturous tunes

Startled the squirrel from its granary,
    And cuckoo flowers fringed the narrow lane,
Through my young leaves a sensuous ecstasy
    Crept like new wine, and every mossy vein
Throbbed with the fitful pulse of amorous blood,
And the wild winds of passion shook my slim stem's maidenhood.

The trooping fawns at evening came and laid

Their cool black noses on my lowest boughs,

And on my topmost branch the blackbird made

   A little nest of grasses for his spouse,

And now and then a twittering wren would light

On a thin twig which hardly bare the weight of such delight.

I was the Attic shepherd's trysting place,

   Beneath my shadow Amaryllis lay,

And round my trunk would laughing Daphnis chase

   The timorous girl, till tired out with play

She felt his hot breath stir her tangled hair,

And turned, and looked, and fled no more from such delightful snare.

Then come away unto my ambuscade

   Where clustering woodbine weaves a canopy

For amorous pleasaunce, and the rustling shade

   Of Paphian myrtles seems to sanctify

The dearest rites of love; there in the cool

And green recesses of its farthest depth there is pool,

The ouzel's haunt, the wild bee's pasturage,

   For round its rim great creamy lilies float

Through their flat leaves in verdant anchorage,

Each cup a white-sailed golden-laden boat

Steered by a dragon-fly,—be not afraid

To leave this wan and wave-kissed shore, surely the place was made

For lovers such as we; the Cyprian Queen,

   One arm around her boyish paramour,

Strays often there at eve, and I have seen

   The moon strip off her misty vestiture

For young Endymion's eyes; be not afraid,

The panther feet of Dian never tread that secret glade.

Nay if thou will'st, back to the beating brine,

   Back to the boisterous billow let us go,

And walk all day beneath the hyaline

   Huge vault of Neptune's watery portico,

And watch the purple monsters of the deep

Sport in ungainly play, and from his lair keen Xiphias leap.

For if my mistress find me lying here

   She will not ruth or gentle pity show,

But lay her boar-spear down, and with austere

   Relentless fingers string the cornel bow,

And draw the feathered notch against her breast,

And loose the archèd cord; aye, even now upon the quest

I hear her hurrying feet,—awake, awake,

    Thou laggard in love's battle! once at least

Let me drink deep of passion's wine, and slake

    My parchèd being with the nectarous feast

Which even gods affect! O come, Love, come,

Still we have time to reach the cavern of thine azure home.'

Scarce had she spoken when the shuddering trees

    Shook, and the leaves divided, and the air

Grew conscious of a god, and the grey seas

    Crawled backward, and a long and dismal blare

Blew from some tasselled horn, a sleuth-hound bayed,

And like a flame a barbèd reed flew whizzing down the glade.

And where the little flowers of her breast

    Just brake into their milky blossoming,

This murderous paramour, this unbidden guest,

    Pierced and struck deep in horrid chambering,

And ploughed a bloody furrow with its dart,

And dug a long red road, and cleft with wingèd death her heart.

Sobbing her life out with a bitter cry

On the boy's body fell the Dryad maid,

Sobbing for incomplete virginity,

   And raptures unenjoyed, and pleasures dead,

And all the pain of things unsatisfied,

And the bright drops of crimson youth crept down her throbbing side.

Ah! pitiful it was to hear her moan,

   And very pitiful to see her die

Ere she had yielded up her sweets, or known

   The joy of passion, that dread mystery

Which not to know is not to live at all,

And yet to know is to be held in death's most deadly thrall.

But as it hapt the Queen of Cythere,

   Who with Adonis all night long had lain

Within some shepherd's hut in Arcady,

   On team of silver doves and gilded wain

Was journeying Paphos-ward, high up afar

From mortal ken between the mountains and the morning star,

And when low down she spied the hapless pair,

   And heard the Oread's faint despairing cry,

Whose cadence seemed to play upon the air

As though it were a viol, hastily

She bade her pigeons fold each straining plume,

And dropt to earth, and reached the strand, and saw their dolorous doom.

For as a gardener turning back his head

   To catch the last notes of the linnet, mows

With careless scythe too near some flower bed,

   And cuts the thorny pillar of the rose,

And with the flower's loosened loneliness

Strews the brown mould; or as some shepherd lad in wantonness

Driving his little flock along the mead

   Treads down two daffodils, which side by aide

Have lured the lady-bird with yellow brede

   And made the gaudy moth forget its pride,

Treads down their brimming golden chalices

Under light feet which were not made for such rude ravages;

Or as a schoolboy tired of his book

   Flings himself down upon the reedy grass

And plucks two water-lilies from the brook,

   And for a time forgets the hour glass,

Then wearies of their sweets, and goes his way,

And lets the hot sun kill them, even go these lovers lay.

And Venus cried, 'It is dread Artemis

   Whose bitter hand hath wrought this cruelty,

Or else that mightier maid whose care it is

   To guard her strong and stainless majesty

Upon the hill Athenian,—alas!

That they who loved so well unloved into Death's house should pass.'

So with soft hands she laid the boy and girl

   In the great golden waggon tenderly

(Her white throat whiter than a moony pearl

   Just threaded with a blue vein's tapestry

Had not yet ceased to throb, and still her breast

Swayed like a wind-stirred lily in ambiguous unrest)

And then each pigeon spread its milky van,

   The bright car soared into the dawning sky,

And like a cloud the aerial caravan

   Passed over the Ægean silently,

Till the faint air was troubled with the song

From the wan mouths that call on bleeding Thammuz all night long.

But when the doves had reached their wonted goal

Where the wide stair of orbèd marble dips

Its snows into the sea, her fluttering soul

    Just shook the trembling petals of her lips

And passed into the void, and Venus knew

That one fair maid the less would walk amid her retinue,

And bade her servants carve a cedar chest

    With all the wonder of this history,

Within whose scented womb their limbs should rest

    Where olive-trees make tender the blue sky

On the low hills of Paphos, and the Faun

Pipes in the noonday, and the nightingale sings on till dawn.

Nor failed they to obey her hest, and ere

    The morning bee had stung the daffodil

With tiny fretful spear, or from its lair

    The waking stag had leapt across the rill

And roused the ouzel, or the lizard crept

Athwart the sunny rock, beneath the grass their bodies slept.

And when day brake, within that silver shrine

    Fed by the flames of cressets tremulous,

Queen Venus knelt and prayed to Proserpine

That she whose beauty made Death amorous

Should beg a guerdon from her pallid Lord,

And let Desire pass across dread Charon's icy ford.

III

In melancholy moonless Acheron,

   Farm for the goodly earth and joyous day

Where no spring ever buds, nor ripening sun

   Weighs down the apple trees, nor flowery May

Chequers with chestnut blooms the grassy floor,

Where thrushes never sing, and piping linnets mate no more,

There by a dim and dark Lethæan well

   Young Charmides was lying; wearily

He plucked the blossoms from the asphodel,

   And with its little rifled treasury

Strewed the dull waters of the dusky stream,

And watched the white stars founder, and the land was like a dream,

When as he gazed into the watery glass

   And through his brown hair's curly tangles scanned

His own wan face, a shadow seemed to pass

   Across the mirror, and a little hand

Stole into his, and warm lips timidly

Brushed his pale cheeks, and breathed their secret forth into a sigh.

Then turned he round his weary eyes and saw,

And ever nigher still their faces came,

And nigher ever did their young mouths draw

Until they seemed one perfect rose of flame,

And longing arms around her neck he cast,

And felt her throbbing bosom, and his breath came hot and fast,

And all his hoarded sweets were hers to kiss,

And all her maidenhood was his to slay,

And limb to limb in long and rapturous bliss

Their passion waxed and waned,—O why essay

To pipe again of love, too venturous reed!

Enough, enough that Eros laughed upon that flowerless mead.

Too venturous poesy, O why essay

To pipe again of passion! fold thy wings

O'er daring Icarus and bid thy lay

Sleep hidden in the lyre's silent strings

Till thou hast found the old Castalian rill,

Or from the Lesbian waters plucked drowned Sappho's golden quid!

157

Enough, enough that he whose life had been

    A fiery pulse of sin, a splendid shame,

Could in the loveless land of Hades glean

    One scorching harvest from those fields of flame

Where passion walks with naked unshod feet

And is not wounded,—ah! enough that once their lips could meet

In that wild throb when all existences

    Seemed narrowed to one single ecstasy

Which dies through its own sweetness and the stress

    Of too much pleasure, ere Persephone

Had bade them serve her by the ebon throne

Of the pale God who in the fields of Enna loosed her zone.

POEMS

REQUIESCAT

Tread lightly, she is near
   Under the snow,
Speak gently, she can hear
   The daisies grow.

All her bright golden hair
   Tarnished with rust,
She that was young and fair
   Fallen to dust.

Lily-like, white as snow,
   She hardly knew
She was a woman, so
   Sweetly she grew.

Coffin-board, heavy stone,
   Lie on her breast,
I vex my heart alone,

She is at rest.

Peace, Peace, she cannot hear
  Lyre or sonnet,
All my life's buried here,
  Heap earth upon it.

Avignon

SAN MINIATO

See, I have climbed the mountain side
   Up to this holy house of God,
   Where once that Angel-Painter trod
Who saw the heavens opened wide,

And throned upon the crescent moon
   The Virginal white Queen of Grace,—
   Mary! could I but see thy face
Death could not come at all too soon.

O crowned by God with thorns and pain!
   Mother of Christ! O mystic wife!
   My heart is weary of this life
And over-sad to sing again.

O crowned by God with love and flame!
   O crowned by Christ the Holy One!
   O listen ere the searching sun
Show to the world my sin and shame.

ROME UNVISITED

I.

The corn has turned from grey to red,
   Since first my spirit wandered forth
   From the drear cities of the north,
And to Italia's mountains fled.

And here I set my face towards home,
   For all my pilgrimage is done,
   Although, methinks, yon blood-red sun
Marshals the way to Holy Rome.

O Blessed Lady, who dost hold
   Upon the seven hills thy reign!
   O Mother without blot or stain,
Crowned with bright crowns of triple gold!

O Roma, Roma, at thy feet
   I lay this barren gift of song!
   For, ah! the way is steep and long
That leads unto thy sacred street.

II.

And yet what joy it were for me
  To turn my feet unto the south,
  And journeying towards the Tiber mouth
To kneel again at Fiesole!

And wandering through the tangled pines
  That break the gold of Arno's stream,
  To see the purple mist and gleam
Of morning on the Apennines

By many a vineyard-hidden home,
  Orchard and olive-garden grey,
  Till from the drear Campagna's way
The seven hills bear up the dome!

III.

A pilgrim from the northern seas—
  What joy for me to seek alone
  The wondrous temple and the throne
Of him who holds the awful keys!

When, bright with purple and with gold
   Come priest and holy cardinal,
   And borne above the heads of all
The gentle Shepherd of the Fold.

O joy to see before I die
   The only God-anointed king,
   And hear the silver trumpets ring
A triumph as he passes by!

Or at the brazen-pillared shrine
   Holds high the mystic sacrifice,
   And shows his God to human eyes
Beneath the veil of bread and wine.

IV.

For lo, what changes time can bring!
   The cycles of revolving years
   May free my heart from all its fears,
And teach my lips a song to sing.

Before yon field of trembling gold

Is garnered into dusty sheaves,

Or ere the autumn's scarlet leaves

Flutter as birds adown the wold,

I may have run the glorious race,

And caught the torch while yet aflame,

And called upon the holy name

Of Him who now doth hide His face.

ARONA

HUMANITAD

It is full winter now: the trees are bare,
  Save where the cattle huddle from the cold
Beneath the pine, for it doth never wear
  The autumn's gaudy livery whose gold
Her jealous brother pilfers, but is true
To the green doublet; bitter is the wind, as though it blew

From Saturn's cave; a few thin wisps of hay
  Lie on the sharp black hedges, where the wain
Dragged the sweet pillage of a summer's day
  From the low meadows up the narrow lane;
Upon the half-thawed snow the bleating sheep
Press close against the hurdles, and the shivering house-dogs creep

From the shut stable to the frozen stream
  And back again disconsolate, and miss
The bawling shepherds and the noisy team;
  And overhead in circling listlessness
The cawing rooks whirl round the frosted stack,
Or crowd the dripping boughs; and in the fen the ice-pools crack

Where the gaunt bittern stalks among the reeds
   And flaps his wings, and stretches back his neck,
And hoots to see the moon; across the meads
   Limps the poor frightened hare, a little speck;
And a stray seamew with its fretful cry
Flits like a sudden drift of snow against the dull grey sky.

Full winter: and the lusty goodman brings
   His load of faggots from the chilly byre,
And stamps his feet upon the hearth, and flings
   The sappy billets on the waning fire,
And laughs to see the sudden lightening scare
His children at their play, and yet,—the spring is in the air;

Already the slim crocus stirs the snow,
   And soon yon blanchèd fields will bloom again
With nodding cowslips for some lad to mow,
   For with the first warm kisses of the rain
The winter's icy sorrow breaks to tears,
And the brown thrushes mate, and with bright eyes the rabbit peers

From the dark warren where the fir-cones lie,

And treads one snowdrop under foot, and runs

Over the mossy knoll, and blackbirds fly

   Across our path at evening, and the suns

Stay longer with us; ah! how good to see

Grass-girdled spring in all her joy of laughing greenery

Dance through the hedges till the early rose,

   (That sweet repentance of the thorny briar!)

Burst from its sheathèd emerald and disclose

   The little quivering disk of golden fire

Which the bees know so well, for with it come

Pale boy's-love, sops-in-wine, and daffadillies all in bloom.

Then up and down the field the sower goes,

   While close behind the laughing younker scares

With shrilly whoop the black and thievish crows,

   And then the chestnut-tree its glory wears,

And on the grass the creamy blossom falls

In odorous excess, and faint half-whispered madrigals

Steal from the bluebells' nodding carillons

   Each breezy morn, and then white jessamine,

That star of its own heaven, snap-dragons

With lolling crimson tongues, and eglantine

In dusty velvets clad usurp the bed

And woodland empery, and when the lingering rose hath shed

Red leaf by leaf its folded panoply,

   And pansies closed their purple-lidded eyes,

Chrysanthemums from gilded argosy

   Unload their gaudy scentless merchandise,

And violets getting overbold withdraw

From their shy nooks, and scarlet berries dot the leafless haw.

O happy field! and O thrice happy tree!

   Soon will your queen in daisy-flowered smock

And crown of flower-de-luce trip down the lea,

   Soon will the lazy shepherds drive their flock

Back to the pasture by the pool, and soon

Through the green leaves will float the hum of murmuring bees at noon.

Soon will the glade be bright with bellamour,

   The flower which wantons love, and those sweet nuns

Vale-lilies in their snowy vestiture

   Will tell their beaded pearls, and carnations

With mitred dusky leaves will scent the wind,

And straggling traveller's-joy each hedge with yellow stars will bind.

Dear bride of Nature and most bounteous spring,
   That canst give increase to the sweet-breath'd kine,
And to the kid its little horns, and bring
   The soft and silky blossoms to the vine,
Where is that old nepenthe which of yore
Man got from poppy root and glossy-berried mandragore!

There was a time when any common bird
   Could make me sing in unison, a time
When all the strings of boyish life were stirred
   To quick response or more melodious rhyme
By every forest idyll;—do I change?
Or rather doth some evil thing through thy fair pleasaunce range?

Nay, nay, thou art the same: 'tis I who seek
   To vex with sighs thy simple solitude,
And because fruitless tears bedew my cheek
   Would have thee weep with me in brotherhood;
Fool! shall each wronged and restless spirit dare
To taint such wine with the salt poison of own despair!

Thou art the same: 'tis I whose wretched soul

Takes discontent to be its paramour,

And gives its kingdom to the rude control

Of what should be its servitor,—for sure

Wisdom is somewhere, though the stormy sea

Contain it not, and the huge deep answer ''Tis not in me.'

To burn with one clear flame, to stand erect

In natural honour, not to bend the knee

In profitless prostrations whose effect

Is by itself condemned, what alchemy

Can teach me this? what herb Medea brewed

Will bring the unexultant peace of essence not subdued?

The minor chord which ends the harmony,

And for its answering brother waits in vain

Sobbing for incompleted melody,

Dies a swan's death; but I the heir of pain,

A silent Memnon with blank lidless eyes,

Wait for the light and music of those suns which never rise.

The quenched-out torch, the lonely cypress-gloom,

The little dust stored in the narrow urn,

The gentle XAIPE of the Attic tomb,—

Were not these better far than to return

To my old fitful restless malady,

Or spend my days within the voiceless cave of misery?

Nay! for perchance that poppy-crownèd god

Is like the watcher by a sick man's bed

Who talks of sleep but gives it not; his rod

Hath lost its virtue, and, when all is said,

Death is too rude, too obvious a key

To solve one single secret in a life's philosophy.

And Love! that noble madness, whose august

And inextinguishable might can slay

The soul with honeyed drugs,—alas! I must

From such sweet ruin play the runaway,

Although too constant memory never can

Forget the archèd splendour of those brows Olympian

Which for a little season made my youth

So soft a swoon of exquisite indolence

That all the chiding of more prudent Truth

Seemed the thin voice of jealousy,—O hence

Thou huntress deadlier than Artemis!

Go seek some other quarry! for of thy too perilous bliss.

My lips have drunk enough,—no more, no more,—
  Though Love himself should turn his gilded prow
Back to the troubled waters of this shore
  Where I am wrecked and stranded, even now
The chariot wheels of passion sweep too near,
Hence! Hence! I pass unto a life more barren, more austere.

More barren—ay, those arms will never lean
  Down through the trellised vines and draw my soul
In sweet reluctance through the tangled green;
  Some other head must wear that aureole,
For I am hers who loves not any man
Whose white and stainless bosom bears the sign Gorgonian.

Let Venus go and chuck her dainty page,
  And kiss his mouth, and toss his curly hair,
With net and spear and hunting equipage
  Let young Adonis to his tryst repair,
But me her fond and subtle-fashioned spell
Delights no more, though I could win her dearest citadel.

Ay, though I were that laughing shepherd boy

Who from Mount Ida saw the little cloud

Pass over Tenedos and lofty Troy

    And knew the coming of the Queen, and bowed

In wonder at her feet, not for the sake

Of a new Helen would I bid her hand the apple take.

Then rise supreme Athena argent-limbed!

    And, if my lips be musicless, inspire

At least my life: was not thy glory hymned

    By One who gave to thee his sword and lyre

Like Æschylos at well-fought Marathon,

And died to show that Milton's England still could bear a son!

And yet I cannot tread the Portico

    And live without desire, fear and pain,

Or nurture that wise calm which long ago

    The grave Athenian master taught to men,

Self-poised, self-centred, and self-comforted,

To watch the world's vain phantasies go by with unbowed head.

Alas! that serene brow, those eloquent lips,

    Those eyes that mirrored all eternity,

Rest in their own Colonos, an eclipse

Hath come on Wisdom, and Mnemosyne

Is childless; in the night which she had made

For lofty secure flight Athena's owl itself hath strayed.

Nor much with Science do I care to climb,

   Although by strange and subtle witchery

She drew the moon from heaven: the Muse Time

   Unrolls her gorgeous-coloured tapestry

To no less eager eyes; often indeed

In the great epic of Polymnia's scroll I love to read

How Asia sent her myriad hosts to war

   Against a little town, and panoplied

In gilded mail with jewelled scimitar,

   White-shielded, purple-crested, rode the Mede

Between the waving poplars and the sea

Which men call Artemisium, till he saw Thermopylæ

Its steep ravine spanned by a narrow wall,

   And on the nearer side a little brood

Of careless lions holding festival!

   And stood amazèd at such hardihood,

And pitched his tent upon the reedy shore,

And stayed two days to wonder, and then crept at midnight o'er

Some unfrequented height, and coming down
   The autumn forests treacherously slew
What Sparta held most dear and was the crown
   Of far Eurotas, and passed on, nor knew
How God had staked an evil net for him
In the small bay at Salamis,—and yet, the page grows dim,

Its cadenced Greek delights me not, I feel
   With such a goodly time too out of tune
To love it much: for like the Dial's wheel
   That from its blinded darkness strikes the noon
Yet never sees the sun, so do my eyes
Restlessly follow that which from my cheated vision flies.

O for one grand unselfish simple life
   To teach us what is Wisdom! speak ye hills
Of lone Helvellyn, for this note of strife
   Shunned your untroubled crags and crystal rills,
Where is that Spirit which living blamelessly
Yet dared to kiss the smitten mouth of his own century!

Speak ye Rydalian laurels! where is he

Whose gentle head ye sheltered, that pure soul

Whose gracious days of uncrowned majesty

    Through lowliest conduct touched the lofty goal

Where love and duty mingle! Him at least

The most high Laws were glad of, he had sat at Wisdom's feast;

But we are Learning's changelings, know by rote

    The clarion watchword of each Grecian school

And follow none, the flawless sword which smote

    The pagan Hydra is an effete tool

Which we ourselves have blunted, what man now

Shall scale the august ancient heights and to old Reverence bow?

One such indeed I saw, but, Ichabod!

    Gone is that last dear son of Italy,

Who being man died for the sake of God,

    And whose unrisen bones sleep peacefully,

O guard him, guard him well, my Giotto's tower,

Thou marble lily of the lily town! let not the lour

Of the rude tempest vex his slumber, or

    The Arno with its tawny troubled gold

O'er-leap its marge, no mightier conqueror

Clomb the high Capitol in the days of old

When Rome was indeed Rome, for Liberty

Walked like a bride beside him, at which sight pale Mystery

Fled shrieking to her farthest sombrest cell

  With an old man who grabbled rusty keys,

Fled shuddering, for that immemorial knell

  With which oblivion buries dynasties

Swept like a wounded eagle on the blast,

As to the holy heart of Rome the great triumvir passed.

He knew the holiest heart and heights of Rome,

  He drave the base wolf from the lion's lair,

And now lies dead by that empyreal dome

  Which overtops Valdarno hung in air

By Brunelleschi—O Melpomene

Breathe through thy melancholy pipe thy sweetest threnody!

Breathe through the tragic stops such melodies

  That Joy's self may grow jealous, and the Nine

Forget awhile their discreet emperies,

  Mourning for him who on Rome's lordliest shrine

Lit for men's lives the light of Marathon,

And bare to sun-forgotten fields the fire of the sun!

O guard him, guard him well, my Giotto's tower!

   Let some young Florentine each eventide

Bring coronals of that enchanted flower

   Which the dim woods of Vallombrosa hide,

And deck the marble tomb wherein he lies

Whose soul is as some mighty orb unseen of mortal eyes;

Some mighty orb whose cycled wanderings,

   Being tempest-driven to the farthest rim

Where Chaos meets Creation and the wings

   Of the eternal chanting Cherubim

Are pavilioned on Nothing, passed away

Into a moonless void,—and yet, though he is dust and clay,

He is not dead, the immemorial Fates

   Forbid it, and the closing shears refrain.

Lift up your heads ye everlasting gates!

   Ye argent clarions, sound a loftier strain

For the vile thing he hated lurks within

Its sombre house, alone with God and memories of sin.

Still what avails it that she sought her cave

That murderous mother of red harlotries?

At Munich on the marble architrave

 The Grecian boys die smiling, but the seas

Which wash Ægina fret in loneliness

Not mirroring their beauty; so our lives grow colourless

For lack of our ideals, if one star

 Flame torch-like in the heavens the unjust

Swift daylight kills it, and no trump of war

 Can wake to passionate voice the silent dust

Which was Mazzini once! rich Niobe

For all her stony sorrows hath her sons; but Italy,

What Easter Day shall make her children rise,

 Who were not Gods yet suffered? what sure feet

Shall find their grave-clothes folded? what clear eyes

 Shall see them bodily? O it were meet

To roll the stone from off the sepulchre

And kiss the bleeding roses of their wounds, in love of her,

Our Italy! our mother visible!

 Most blessed among nations and most sad,

For whose dear sake the young Calabrian fell

That day at Aspromonte and was glad

That in an age when God was bought and sold

One man could die for Liberty! but we, burnt out and cold,

See Honour smitten on the cheek and gyves

    Bind the sweet feet of Mercy: Poverty

Creeps through our sunless lanes and with sharp knives

    Cuts the warm throats of children stealthily,

And no word said:—O we are wretched men

Unworthy of our great inheritance! where is the pen

Of austere Milton? where the mighty sword

    Which slew its master righteously? the years

Have lost their ancient leader, and no word

    Breaks from the voiceless tripod on our ears:

While as a ruined mother in some spasm

Bears a base child and loathes it, so our best enthusiasm

Genders unlawful children, Anarchy

    Freedom's own Judas, the vile prodigal

Licence who steals the gold of Liberty

    And yet has nothing, Ignorance the real

One Fraticide since Cain, Envy the asp

That stings itself to anguish, Avarice whose palsied grasp

Is in its extent stiffened, moneyed Greed

   For whose dull appetite men waste away

Amid the whirr of wheels and are the seed

   Of things which slay their sower, these each day

Sees rife in England, and the gentle feet

Of Beauty tread no more the stones of each unlovely street.

What even Cromwell spared is desecrated

   By weed and worm, left to the stormy play

Of wind and beating snow, or renovated

   By more destructful hands: Time's worst decay

Will wreathe its ruins with some loveliness,

But these new Vandals can but make a rain-proof barrenness.

Where is that Art which bade the Angels sing

   Through Lincoln's lofty choir, till the air

Seems from such marble harmonies to ring

   With sweeter song than common lips can dare

To draw from actual reed? ah! where is now

The cunning hand which made the flowering hawthorn branches bow

For Southwell's arch, and carved the House of One

Who loved the lilies of the field with all

Our dearest English flowers? the same sun

    Rises for us: the seasons natural

Weave the same tapestry of green and grey:

The unchanged hills are with us: but that Spirit hath passed away.

And yet perchance it may be better so,

    For Tyranny is an incestuous Queen,

Murder her brother is her bedfellow,

    And the Plague chambers with her: in obscene

And bloody paths her treacherous feet are set;

Better the empty desert and a soul inviolate!

For gentle brotherhood, the harmony

    Of living in the healthful air, the swift

Clean beauty of strong limbs when men are free

    And women chaste, these are the things which lift

Our souls up more than even Agnolo's

Gaunt blinded Sibyl poring o'er the scroll of human woes,

Or Titian's little maiden on the stair

    White as her own sweet lily and as tall,

Or Mona Lisa smiling through her hair,—

Ah! somehow life is bigger after all

Than any painted angel, could we see

The God that is within us! The old Greek serenity

Which curbs the passion of that level line

   Of marble youths, who with untroubled eyes

And chastened limbs ride round Athena's shrine

   And mirror her divine economies,

And balanced symmetry of what in man

Would else wage ceaseless warfare,—this at least within the span

Between our mother's kisses and the grave

   Might so inform our lives, that we could win

Such mighty empires that from her cave

   Temptation would grow hoarse, and pallid Sin

Would walk ashamed of his adulteries,

And Passion creep from out the House of Lust with startled eyes.

To make the body and the spirit one

   With all right things, till no thing live in vain

From morn to noon, but in sweet unison

   With every pulse of flesh and throb of brain

The soul in flawless essence high enthroned,

Against all outer vain attack invincibly bastioned,

Mark with serene impartiality
  The strife of things, and yet be comforted,
Knowing that by the chain causality
  All separate existences are wed
Into one supreme whole, whose utterance
Is joy, or holier praise! ah! surely this were governance

Of Life in most august omnipresence,
  Through which the rational intellect would find
In passion its expression, and mere sense,
  Ignoble else, lend fire to the mind,
And being joined with it in harmony
More mystical than that which binds the stars planetary,

Strike from their several tones one octave chord
  Whose cadence being measureless would fly
Through all the circling spheres, then to its Lord
  Return refreshed with its new empery
And more exultant power,—this indeed
Could we but reach it were to find the last, the perfect creed.

Ah! it was easy when the world was young

185

To keep one's life free and inviolate,

From our sad lips another song is rung,

   By our own hands our heads are desecrate,

Wanderers in drear exile, and dispossessed

Of what should be our own, we can but feed on wild unrest.

Somehow the grace, the bloom of things has flown,

   And of all men we are most wretched who

Must live each other's lives and not our own

   For very pity's sake and then undo

All that we lived for—it was otherwise

When soul and body seemed to blend in mystic symphonies.

But we have left those gentle haunts to pass

   With weary feet to the new Calvary,

Where we behold, as one who in a glass

   Sees his own face, self-slain Humanity,

And in the dumb reproach of that sad gaze

Learn what an awful phantom the red hand of man can raise.

O smitten mouth! O forehead crowned with thorn!

   O chalice of all common miseries!

Thou for our sakes that loved thee not hast borne

An agony of endless centuries,

And we were vain and ignorant nor knew

That when we stabbed thy heart it was our own real hearts we slew.

Being ourselves the sowers and the seeds,

  The night that covers and the lights that fade,

The spear that pierces and the side that bleeds,

  The lips betraying and the life betrayed;

The deep hath calm: the moon hath rest: but we

Lords of the natural world are yet our own dread enemy.

Is this the end of all that primal force

  Which, in its changes being still the same,

From eyeless Chaos cleft its upward course,

  Through ravenous seas and whirling rocks and flame,

Till the suns met in heaven and began

Their cycles, and the morning stars sang, and the Word was Man!

Nay, nay, we are but crucified, and though

  The bloody sweat falls from our brows like rain

Loosen the nails—we shall come down I know,

  Staunch the red wounds—we shall be whole again,

No need have we of hyssop-laden rod,

That which is purely human, that is godlike, that is God.

LOUIS NAPOLEON

Eagle of Austerlitz! where were thy wings
  When far away upon a barbarous strand,
  In fight unequal, by an obscure hand,
Fell the last scion of thy brood of Kings!

Poor boy! thou shalt not flaunt thy cloak of red,
  Or ride in state through Paris in the van
  Of thy returning legions, but instead
Thy mother France, free and republican,

Shall on thy dead and crownless forehead place
  The better laurels of a soldier's crown,
  That not dishonoured should thy soul go down
To tell the mighty Sire of thy race

That France hath kissed the mouth of Liberty,
  And found it sweeter than his honied bees,
  And that the giant wave Democracy
Breaks on the shores where Kings lay couched at ease.

ENDYMION

(FOR MUSIC)

The apple trees are hung with gold,
   And birds are loud in Arcady,
The sheep lie bleating in the fold,
The wild goat runs across the wold,
But yesterday his love he told,
   I know he will come back to me.
O rising moon! O Lady moon!
   Be you my lover's sentinel,
   You cannot choose but know him well,
For he is shod with purple shoon,
You cannot choose but know my love,
   For he a shepherd's crook doth bear,
And he is soft as any dove,
   And brown and curly is his hair.

The turtle now has ceased to call
   Upon her crimson-footed groom,
The grey wolf prowls about the stall,
The lily's singing seneschal
Sleeps in the lily-bell, and all

The violet hills are lost in gloom.

O risen moon! O holy moon!

  Stand on the top of Helice,

  And if my own true love you see,

Ah! if you see the purple shoon,

The hazel crook, the lad's brown hair,

  The goat-skin wrapped about his arm,

Tell him that I am waiting where

  The rushlight glimmers in the Farm.

The falling dew is cold and chill,

  And no bird sings in Arcady,

The little fauns have left the hill,

Even the tired daffodil

Has closed its gilded doors, and still

  My lover comes not back to me.

False moon! False moon! O waning moon!

  Where is my own true lover gone,

  Where are the lips vermilion,

The shepherd's crook, the purple shoon?

Why spread that silver pavilion,

  Why wear that veil of drifting mist?

Ah! thou hast young Endymion

  Thou hast the lips that should be kissed!

LE JARDIN

The lily's withered chalice falls
   Around its rod of dusty gold,
   And from the beech-trees on the wold
The last wood-pigeon coos and calls.

The gaudy leonine sunflower
   Hangs black and barren on its stalk,
   And down the windy garden walk
The dead leaves scatter,—hour by hour.

Pale privet-petals white as milk
   Are blown into a snowy mass:
   The roses lie upon the grass
Like little shreds of crimson silk.

LA MER

A white mist drifts across the shrouds,
  A wild moon in this wintry sky
  Gleams like an angry lion's eye
Out of a mane of tawny clouds.

The muffled steersman at the wheel
  Is but a shadow in the gloom;—
  And in the throbbing engine-room
Leap the long rods of polished steel.

The shattered storm has left its trace
  Upon this huge and heaving dome,
  For the thin threads of yellow foam
Float on the waves like ravelled lace.

LE PANNEAU

Under the rose-tree's dancing shade
    There stands a little ivory girl,
    Pulling the leaves of pink and pearl
With pale green nails of polished jade.

The red leaves fall upon the mould,
    The white leaves flutter, one by one,
    Down to a blue bowl where the sun,
Like a great dragon, writhes in gold.

The white leaves float upon the air,
    The red leaves flutter idly down,
    Some fall upon her yellow gown,
And some upon her raven hair.

She takes an amber lute and sings,
    And as she sings a silver crane
    Begins his scarlet neck to strain,
And flap his burnished metal wings.

She takes a lute of amber bright,

And from the thicket where he lies
Her lover, with his almond eyes,
Watches her movements in delight.

And now she gives a cry of fear,
    And tiny tears begin to start:
    A thorn has wounded with its dart
The pink-veined sea-shell of her ear.

And now she laughs a merry note:
    There has fallen a petal of the rose
    Just where the yellow satin shows
The blue-veined flower of her throat.

With pale green nails of polished jade,
    Pulling the leaves of pink and pearl,
    There stands a little ivory girl
Under the rose-tree's dancing shade.

LES BALLONS

Against these turbid turquoise skies
    The light and luminous balloons
    Dip and drift like satin moons
Drift like silken butterflies;

Reel with every windy gust,
    Rise and reel like dancing girls,
    Float like strange transparent pearls,
Fall and float like silver dust.

Now to the low leaves they cling,
    Each with coy fantastic pose,
    Each a petal of a rose
Straining at a gossamer string.

Then to the tall trees they climb,
    Like thin globes of amethyst,
    Wandering opals keeping tryst
With the rubies of the lime.

CANZONET

I have no store
Of gryphon-guarded gold;
  Now, as before,
Bare is the shepherd's fold.
  Rubies nor pearls
Have I to gem thy throat;
  Yet woodland girls
Have loved the shepherd's note.

  Then pluck a reed
And bid me sing to thee,
  For I would feed
Thine ears with melody,
  Who art more fair
Than fairest fleur-de-lys,
  More sweet and rare
Than sweetest ambergris.

  What dost thou fear?
Young Hyacinth is slain,
  Pan is not here,

And will not come again.

   No horned Faun

Treads down the yellow leas,

   No God at dawn

Steals through the olive trees.

   Hylas is dead,

Nor will he e'er divine

   Those little red

Rose-petalled lips of thine.

   On the high hill

No ivory dryads play,

   Silver and still

Sinks the sad autumn day.

LE JARDIN DES TUILERIES

This winter air is keen and cold,
    And keen and cold this winter sun,
    But round my chair the children run
Like little things of dancing gold.

Sometimes about the painted kiosk
    The mimic soldiers strut and stride,
    Sometimes the blue-eyed brigands hide
In the bleak tangles of the bosk.

And sometimes, while the old nurse cons
    Her book, they steal across the square,
    And launch their paper navies where
Huge Triton writhes in greenish bronze.

And now in mimic flight they flee,
    And now they rush, a boisterous band—
    And, tiny hand on tiny hand,
Climb up the black and leafless tree.

Ah! cruel tree! if I were you,

And children climbed me, for their sake

Though it be winter I would break

Into spring blossoms white and blue!

PAN: DOUBLE VILLANELLE

I.

O goat-foot God of Arcady!

This modern world is grey and old,

And what remains to us of thee?

No more the shepherd lads in glee

Throw apples at thy wattled fold,

O goat-foot God of Arcady!

Nor through the laurels can one see

Thy soft brown limbs, thy beard of gold

And what remains to us of thee?

And dull and dead our Thames would be,

For here the winds are chill and cold,

O goat-loot God of Arcady!

Then keep the tomb of Helice,

Thine olive-woods, thy vine-clad wold,

And what remains to us of thee?

Though many an unsung elegy

Sleeps in the reeds our rivers hold,

O goat-foot God of Arcady!

Ah, what remains to us of thee?

II.

Ah, leave the hills of Arcady,

Thy satyrs and their wanton play,

This modern world hath need of thee.

No nymph or Faun indeed have we,

For Faun and nymph are old and grey,

Ah, leave the hills of Arcady!

This is the land where liberty

Lit grave-browed Milton on his way,

This modern world hath need of thee!

A land of ancient chivalry

Where gentle Sidney saw the day,

Ah, leave the hills of Arcady!

This fierce sea-lion of the sea,

This England lacks some stronger lay,

This modern world hath need of thee!

Then blow some trumpet loud and free,

And give thine oaten pipe away,

Ah, leave the hills of Arcady!

This modern world hath need of thee!

IN THE FOREST

Out of the mid-wood's twilight
  Into the meadow's dawn,
Ivory limbed and brown-eyed,
  Flashes my Faun!

He skips through the copses singing,
  And his shadow dances along,
And I know not which I should follow,
  Shadow or song!

O Hunter, snare me his shadow!
  O Nightingale, catch me his strain!
Else moonstruck with music and madness
  I track him in vain!

SYMPHONY IN YELLOW

An omnibus across the bridge
   Crawls like a yellow butterfly
   And, here and there, a passer-by
Shows like a little restless midge.

Big barges full of yellow hay
   Are moored against the shadowy wharf,
   And, like a yellow silken scarf,
The thick fog hangs along the quay.

The yellow leaves begin to fade
   And flutter from the Temple elms,
   And at my feet the pale green Thames
Lies like a rod of rippled jade.

SONNETS

HÉLAS!

To drift with every passion till my soul

Is a stringed lute on which can winds can play,

Is it for this that I have given away

Mine ancient wisdom and austere control?

Methinks my life is a twice-written scroll

Scrawled over on some boyish holiday

With idle songs for pipe and virelay,

Which do but mar the secret of the whole.

Surely there was a time I might have trod

The sunlit heights, and from life's dissonance

Struck one clear chord to reach the ears of God:

Is that time dead? lo! with a little rod

I did but touch the honey of romance—

And must I lose a soul's inheritance?

TO MILTON

Milton! I think thy spirit hath passed away

From these white cliffs and high-embattled towers;

This gorgeous fiery-coloured world of ours

Seems fallen into ashes dull and grey,

And the age changed unto a mimic play

Wherein we waste our else too-crowded hours:

For all our pomp and pageantry and powers

We are but fit to delve the common clay,

Seeing this little isle on which we stand,

This England, this sea-lion of the sea,

By ignorant demagogues is held in fee,

Who love her not: Dear God! is this the land

Which bare a triple empire in her hand

When Cromwell spake the word Democracy!

ON THE MASSACRE OF THE CHRISTIANS IN BULGARIA

Christ, dost Thou live indeed? or are Thy bones

Still straitened in their rock-hewn sepulchre?

And was Thy Rising only dreamed by her

Whose love of Thee for all her sin atones?

For here the air is horrid with men's groans,

The priests who call upon Thy name are slain,

Dost Thou not hear the bitter wail of pain

From those whose children lie upon the stones?

Come down, O Son of God! incestuous gloom

Curtains the land, and through the starless night

Over Thy Cross a Crescent moon I see!

If Thou in very truth didst burst the tomb

Come down, O Son of Man! and show Thy might

Lest Mahomet be crowned instead of Thee!

HOLY WEEK AT GENOA

I wandered through Scoglietto's far retreat,

   The oranges on each o'erhanging spray

   Burned as bright lamps of gold to shame the day;

Some startled bird with fluttering wings and fleet

Made snow of all the blossoms; at my feet

   Like silver moons the pale narcissi lay:

   And the curved waves that streaked the great green bay

Laughed i' the sun, and life seemed very sweet.

Outside the young boy-priest passed singing clear,

   'Jesus the son of Mary has been slain,

   O come and fill His sepulchre with flowers.'

Ah, God! Ah, God! those dear Hellenic hours

   Had drowned all memory of Thy bitter pain,

   The Cross, the Crown, the Soldiers and the Spear.

URBS SACRA ÆTERNA

Rome! what a scroll of History thine has been;

   In the first days thy sword republican

   Ruled the whole world for many an age's span:

Then of the peoples wert thou royal Queen,

Till in thy streets the bearded Goth was seen;

   And now upon thy walls the breezes fan

   (Ah, city crowned by God, discrowned by man!)

The hated flag of red and white and green.

When was thy glory! when in search for power

   Thine eagles flew to greet the double sun,

   And the wild nations shuddered at thy rod?

Nay, but thy glory tarried for this hour,

   When pilgrims kneel before the Holy One,

   The prisoned shepherd of the Church of God.

   Montre Mario

E TENEBRIS

Come down, O Christ, and help me! reach Thy hand,

    For I am drowning in a stormier sea

    Than Simon on Thy lake of Galilee:

The wine of life is spilt upon the sand,

My heart is as some famine-murdered land

    Whence all good things have perished utterly,

    And well I know my soul in Hell must lie

If I this night before God's throne should stand.

'He sleeps perchance, or rideth to the chase,

    Like Baal, when his prophets howled that name

    From morn to noon on Carmel's smitten height.'

Nay, peace, I shall behold, before the night,

    The feet of brass, the robe more white than flame,

    The wounded hands, the weary human face.

AT VERONA

How steep the stairs within King's houses are
　　For exile-wearied feet as mine to tread,
　　And O how salt and bitter is the bread
Which falls from this Hound's table,—better far
That I had died in the red ways of war,
　　Or that the gate of Florence bare my head,
　　Than to live thus, by all things comraded
Which seek the essence of my soul to mar.

'Curse God and die: what better hope than this?
　　He hath forgotten thee in all the bliss
　　Of his gold city, and eternal day'—
Nay peace: behind my prison's blinded bars
　　I do possess what none can take away,
　　My love and all the glory of the stars.

ON THE SALE BY AUCTION OF KEATS' LOVE LETTERS

These are the letters which Endymion wrote
  To one he loved in secret, and apart.
  And now the brawlers of the auction mart
Bargain and bid for each poor blotted note,
Ay! for each separate pulse of passion quote
  The merchant's price. I think they love not art
  Who break the crystal of a poet's heart
That small and sickly eyes may glare and gloat.

Is it not said that many years ago,
  In a far Eastern town, some soldiers ran
  With torches through the midnight, and began
To wrangle for mean raiment, and to throw
  Dice for the garments of a wretched man,
Not knowing the God's wonder, or His woe?

THE NEW REMORSE

The sin was mine; I did not understand.

  So now is music prisoned in her cave,

  Save where some ebbing desultory wave

Frets with its restless whirls this meagre strand.

And in the withered hollow of this land

  Hath Summer dug herself so deep a grave,

  That hardly can the leaden willow crave

One silver blossom from keen Winter's hand.

But who is this who cometh by the shore?

(Nay, love, look up and wonder!) Who is this

  Who cometh in dyed garments from the South?

It is thy new-found Lord, and he shall kiss

  The yet unravished roses of thy mouth,

And I shall weep and worship, as before.

CHILDREN IN PRISON AND OTHER CRUELTIES OF PRISON LIFE

PUBLISHERS' NOTE.

The circumstance which called forth this letter is a woeful one for Christian England. Martin, the Reading warder, is found guilty of feeding the hungry, nursing the sick, of being kindly and humane. These are his offences in plain unofficial language.

This pamphlet is tendered to earnest persons as evidence that the prison system is opposed to all that is kind and helpful. Herein is shown a process that is dehumanizing, not only to the prisoners, but to every one connected with it.

Martin was dismissed. It happened in May last year. He is still out of employment and in poor circumstances. Can anyone help him?

February, 1898.

SOME CRUELTIES OF PRISON LIFE.

THE EDITOR OF THE DAILY CHRONICLE.

Sir,—I learn with great regret, through an extract from the columns of your paper, that the warder Martin, of Reading Prison, has been dismissed by the Prison Commissioners for having given some sweet biscuits to a little hungry child. I saw the three children myself on the Monday preceding my release. They had just been convicted, and were standing in a row in the central hall in their prison dress, carrying their sheets under the arms previous to their being sent to the cells allotted to them. I happened to be passing along one of the galleries on my way to the reception room, where I was to have an interview with a friend. They were quite small children, the youngest—the one to whom the warder gave the biscuits—being a tiny little chap, for whom they had evidently been unable to find clothes small enough to fit. I had, of course, seen many children in prison during the two years during which I was myself confined. Wandsworth Prison, especially, contained always a large number of children. But the little child I saw on the afternoon of Monday, the 17th, at Reading, was tinier than any one of them. I need not say how utterly distressed I was to see these children at Reading, for I knew the treatment in store for them. The cruelty that is practised by day and night on children in English prisons is incredible, except to those who have witnessed it and are aware of the brutality of the system.

People nowadays do not understand what cruelty is. They regard it as a sort of terrible mediæval passion, and connect it with the race of men like Eccelin da Romano, and others, to whom the deliberate infliction of pain gave a real madness of pleasure. But men of the stamp of Eccelin are merely abnormal types of perverted individualism. Ordinary cruelty is simply stupidity. It comes from the entire want of imagination. It is the result in our days of stereotyped systems, of hard-and-fast rules, of centralisation, of officialism, and of irresponsible authority. Wherever there is centralisation there is stupidity. What is inhuman in modern life is officialism. Authority is as destructive to those who exercise it as it is to those on whom it is exercised.

It is the Prison Board, with the system that it carries out, that is the primary source of the cruelty that is exercised on a child in prison. The people who uphold the system have excellent intentions. Those who carry it out are humane in intention also. Responsibility is shifted on to the disciplinary regulations. It is supposed that because a thing is the rule it is right.

The present treatment of children is terrible, primarily from people not understanding the peculiar psychology of a child's nature. A child can understand a punishment inflicted by an individual, such as a parent or guardian, and bear it with a certain amount of acquiescence. What it cannot understand is a punishment inflicted by Society. It cannot realise what Society is. With grown people it is, of course, the reverse. Those of us who are either in prison or have been sent there, can understand, and do understand, what that collective force called Society means, and whatever we may think of its methods or claims, we can force ourselves to accept it. Punishment inflicted on us by an individual, on the other hand, is a thing that no grown person endures or is expected to endure.

The child consequently, being taken away from its parents by people whom it has never seen, and of whom it knows nothing, and finding itself in a lonely and unfamiliar cell, waited on by strange faces, and ordered about and punished by the representatives of a system that it cannot understand, becomes an immediate prey to the first and most prominent emotion produced by modern prison life—the emotion of terror. The terror of a child in prison is quite limitless. I remember once in Reading, as I was going out to exercise, seeing in the dimly-lit cell, right opposite my own, a small boy. Two warders, not unkindly men, were talking to him, with some sternness apparently, or perhaps giving him some useful advice about his conduct. One was in the cell with him, the other was standing outside. The child's face was like a white wedge of sheer terror. There was in his eyes the mute appeal of a hunted animal. The next morning I heard him at breakfast-time crying, and calling to be let out. His cry was for his parents. From time to time I could hear the deep voice of the warder on duty warning him to keep quiet. Yet he was not even convicted of whatever little offence he had been charged with. He was simply on remand. That I knew by his wearing his own clothes, which

220

seemed neat enough. He was, however, wearing prison socks and shoes. This showed that he was a very poor boy, whose own shoes, if he had any, were in a bad state. Justices and magistrates, an entirely ignorant class as a rule, often remand children for a week, and then perhaps remit whatever sentence they are entitled to pass. They call this "not sending a child to prison." It is, of course, a stupid view on their part. To a little child, whether he is in prison on remand or after conviction, is a subtlety of social position he cannot comprehend. To him the horrible thing is to be there at all. In the eyes of humanity it should be a horrible thing for him to be there at all.

This terror that seizes and dominates the child, as it seizes the grown man also, is of course intensified beyond power of expression by the solitary cellular system of our prisons. Every child is confined to its cell for twenty-three hours out of the twenty-four. This is the appalling thing. To shut up a child in a dimly-lit cell for twenty-three hours out of the twenty-four is an example of the cruelty of stupidity. If an individual, parent or guardian, did this to a child he would be severely punished. The Society for the Prevention of Cruelty to Children would take the matter up at once. There would be on all hands the utmost detestation of whomsoever had been guilty of such cruelty. A heavy sentence would undoubtedly follow conviction. But our own actual society does worse itself, and to the child to be so treated by a strange abstract force, of whose claims it has no cognizance, is much worse than it would be to receive the same treatment from its father or mother, or someone it knew. The inhuman treatment of a child is always inhuman, by whomsoever it is inflicted. But inhuman treatment by Society is to the child the more terrible because there is no appeal. A parent or guardian can be moved, and let out the child from the dark lonely room in which it is confined. But a warder cannot. Most warders are very fond of children. But the system prohibits them from rendering the child any assistance. Should they do so, as Warder Martin did, they are dismissed.

The second thing from which a child suffers in prison is hunger. The food that is given to it consists of a piece of usually badly-baked prison bread and a tin of water for breakfast at half-past seven. At twelve o'clock it gets dinner, composed of a tin of coarse Indian meal stirabout, and at half-past five it gets a piece of dry bread and a tin of water for its supper. This diet in the case of a strong grown man is always productive of illness of some kind, chiefly of course diarrhœa, with its attendant weakness. In fact in a big prison astringent medicines are served out regularly by the warders as a matter of course. In the case of a child, the child is, as a rule, incapable of eating the food at all. Anyone who knows anything about children knows how easily a child's digestion is upset by a fit of crying, or trouble and mental distress of any kind. A child who has been crying all day long, and perhaps half the night, in a lonely dimly-lit cell, and is preyed upon by terror, simply cannot eat food of this coarse, horrible kind. In the case of the little child to whom Warder Martin gave the biscuits, the child was crying with hunger on Tuesday morning, and utterly unable to eat the bread and water served to it for its breakfast. Martin went out after the breakfasts had been served and bought the few sweet biscuits for the child rather than see it starving. It was a beautiful action on his part, and was so recognised by the child, who, utterly unconscious of the regulation of the Prison Board, told one of the senior warders how kind this junior warder had been to him. The result was, of course, a report and a dismissal.

I know Martin extremely well, and I was under his charge for the last seven weeks of my imprisonment. On his appointment at Reading he had charge of Gallery C, in which I was confined, so I saw him constantly. I was struck by the singular kindness and humanity of the way in which he spoke to me and to the other prisoners. Kind words are much in prison, and a pleasant "Good morning" or "Good evening" will make one as happy as one can be in solitary confinement. He was always gentle and considerate. I happen to know another case in which he showed great kindness to one of the prisoners, and I have no hesitation in mentioning it. One of the most horrible things in prison is the badness of the sanitary arrangements. No prisoner is allowed under any circumstances to leave his cell after half-past five p.m. If, consequently, he is suffering from diarrhœa, he has to use his cell as a latrine, and pass the night in a most fetid and unwholesome atmosphere. Some days before my release Martin was going the rounds at half-past seven with one of the senior warders for the purpose of collecting the oakum and tools of the prisoners. A man just convicted, and suffering from violent diarrhœa in consequence of the food, as is always the case, asked this senior warder to allow him to empty the slops in his cell on account of the horrible odour of the cell and the possibility of illness again in the night. The senior warder refused absolutely; it was against the rules. The man, as far as he was concerned, had to pass the night in this dreadful condition. Martin, however, rather than see this wretched man in such a loathsome predicament, said he would empty the man's slops himself, and did so. A warder emptying a prisoner's slops is, of course, against the rules, but Martin did this act of kindness to the man out of the simple humanity of his nature, and the man was naturally most grateful.

As regards the children, a great deal has been talked and written lately about the contaminating influence of prison on young children. What is said is quite true. A child is utterly contaminated by prison life. But the contaminating influence is not that of the prisoners. It is that of the whole prison system—of the governor, the chaplain, the warders, the lonely cell, the isolation, the revolting food, the rules of the Prison Commissioners, the mode of discipline as it is termed, of the life. Every care is taken to isolate a child from the sight even of all prisoners over sixteen years of age. Children sit behind a curtain in chapel, and are sent to take exercise in small sunless yards—sometimes a stone-yard, sometimes a yard at the back of the mills—rather than that they should see the elder prisoners at exercise. But the only really humanising influence in prison is the influence of the prisoners. Their cheerfulness under terrible circumstances, their sympathy for each other, their humility, their gentleness, their pleasant smiles of greeting when they meet each other, their complete acquiescence in their punishments, are all quite wonderful, and I myself learnt many sound lessons from them. I am not proposing that the children should not sit behind a curtain in chapel, or that they should take exercise in a corner of the common yard. I am merely pointing out that the bad influence on children is not, and could never be, that of the prisoners, but is, and will always remain, that of the prison system itself. There is not a single man in Reading Gaol that would not gladly have done the three children's punishment for them. When I saw them last it was on the Tuesday following their conviction. I was taking exercise at half-past eleven with about twelve other men, as the three children passed near us, in charge of a warder, from the damp, dreary stone-yard in which they had been at their exercise. I saw the greatest pity and sympathy in the eyes of my companions as they looked at them. Prisoners are, as a class, extremely kind and sympathetic to each other. Suffering and the community of suffering makes people kind, and day after day as I tramped the yard I used to feel with pleasure and comfort what Carlyle calls somewhere "the silent rhythmic charm of human companionship." In this as in all other things, philanthropists and people of that kind are astray. It is not the prisoners who need reformation. It is the prisons.

Of course no child under fourteen years of age should be sent to prison at all. It is an absurdity, and, like many absurdities, of absolutely tragic results. If, however, they are to be sent to prison, during the daytime they should be in a workshop or schoolroom with a warder. At night they should sleep in a dormitory, with a night-warder to look after them. They should be allowed exercise for at least three hours a day. The dark, badly-ventilated, ill-smelling prison cells are dreadful for a child, dreadful indeed for anyone. One is always breathing bad air in prison. The food given to children should consist of tea and bread-and-butter and soup. Prison soup is very good and wholesome. A resolution of the House of Commons could settle the treatment of children in half an hour. I hope you will use your influence to have this done. The way that children are treated at present is really an outrage on humanity and common-sense. It comes from stupidity.

Let me draw attention now to another terrible thing that goes on in English prisons, indeed in prisons all over the world where the system of silence and cellular confinement is practised. I refer to the large number of men who become insane or weak-minded in prison. In convict prisons this is, of course, quite common; but in ordinary gaols also, such as that I was confined in, it is to be found.

About three months ago, I noticed amongst the prisoners who took exercise with me a young man who seemed to me to be silly or half-witted. Every prison of course has its half-witted clients, who return again and again, and may be said to live in the prison. But this young man struck me as being more than usually half-witted on account of his silly grin and idiotic laughter to himself, and the peculiar restlessness of his eternally twitching hands. He

224

was noticed by all the other prisoners on account of the strangeness of his conduct. From time to time he did not appear at exercise, which showed me that he was being punished by confinement to his cell. Finally, I discovered that he was under observation, and being watched night and day by warders. When he did appear at exercise, he always seemed hysterical, and used to walk round crying or laughing. At chapel he had to sit right under the observation of two warders, who carefully watched him all the time. Sometimes he would bury his head in his hands, an offence against the chapel regulations, and his head would be immediately struck up by a warder, so that he should keep his eyes fixed permanently in the direction of the Communion-table. Sometimes he would cry—not making any disturbance—but with tears streaming down his face and a hysterical throbbing in the throat. Sometimes he would grin idiot-like to himself and make faces. He was on more than one occasion sent out of chapel to his cell, and of course he was continually punished. As the bench on which I used to sit in chapel was directly behind the bench at the end of which this unfortunate man was placed, I had full opportunity of observing him. I also saw him, of course, at exercise continually, and I saw that he was becoming insane, and was being treated as if he was shamming.

On Saturday week last, I was in my cell at about one o'clock occupied in cleaning and polishing the tins I had been using for dinner. Suddenly I was startled by the prison silence being broken by the most horrible and revolting shrieks or rather howls, for at first I thought some animal like a bull or a cow was being unskilfully slaughtered outside the prison walls. I soon realised, however, that the howls proceeded from the basement of the prison, and I knew that some wretched man was being flogged. I need not say how hideous and terrible it was for me, and I began to wonder who it was who was being punished in this revolting manner. Suddenly it dawned upon me that they might be flogging this unfortunate lunatic. My feelings on the subject need not be chronicled; they have nothing to do with the question.

The next day, Sunday 16th, I saw the poor fellow at exercise, his weak, ugly, wretched face bloated by tears and hysteria almost beyond recognition. He walked in the centre ring along with the old men, the beggars and the lame people, so that I was able to observe him the whole time. It was my last Sunday in prison, a perfectly lovely day, the finest day we had had the whole year, and there, in the beautiful sunlight, walked this poor creature—made once in the image of God—grinning like an ape, and making with his hands the most fantastic gestures, as though he was playing in the air on some invisible stringed instrument, or arranging and dealing counters in some curious game. All the while these hysterical tears, without which none of us ever saw him, were making soiled runnels on his white swollen face. The hideous and deliberate grace of his gestures made him like an antic. He was a living grotesque. The other prisoners all watched him, and not one of them smiled. Everybody knew what had happened to him, and that he was being driven insane—was insane already. After half-an-hour, he was ordered in by the warder, and, I suppose, punished. At least he was not at exercise on Monday, though I think I caught sight of him at the corner of the stone-yard, walking in charge of a warder.

On the Tuesday—my last day in prison—I saw him at exercise. He was worse than before, and again was sent in. Since then I know nothing of him, but I found out from one of the prisoners who walked with me at exercise that he had had twenty-four lashes in the cook-house on Saturday afternoon, by order of the visiting justices on the report of the doctor. The howls that had horrified us all were his.

This man is undoubtedly becoming insane. Prison doctors have no knowledge of mental disease of any kind. They are as a class ignorant men. The pathology of the mind is unknown to them. When a man grows insane, they treat him as shamming. They have him punished again and again. Naturally the man becomes worse. When ordinary punishments are exhausted, the doctor reports the case to the justices. The result is flogging. Of course the flogging is not done with a cat-of-nine-tails. It is what is called birching. The instrument is a rod; but the result on the wretched half-witted man may be imagined.

His number is, or was, A. 2. 11. I also managed to find out his name. It is Prince. Something should be done at once for him. He is a soldier, and his sentence is one of court-martial. The term is six months. Three have yet to run.

226

May I ask you to use your influence to have this case examined into, and to see that the lunatic prisoner is properly treated?

No report by the Medical Commissioners is of any avail. It is not to be trusted. The medical inspectors do not seem to understand the difference between idiocy and lunacy—between the entire absence of a function or organ and the diseases of a function or organ. This man A. 2. 11, will, I have no doubt, be able to tell his name, the nature of his offence, the day of the month, the date of the beginning and expiration of his sentence, and answer any ordinary simple question; but that his mind is diseased admits of no doubt. At present it is a horrible duel between himself and the doctor. The doctor is fighting for a theory. The man is fighting for his life. I am anxious that the man should win. But let the whole case be examined into by experts who understand brain-disease, and by people of humane feelings who have still some common-sense and some pity. There is no reason that the sentimentalist should be asked to interfere. He always does harm. He culminates at his starting point. His end, as his origin, is an emotion.

The case is a special instance of the cruelty inseparable from a stupid system, for the present Governor of Reading is a man of gentle and humane character, greatly liked and respected by all the prisoners. He was appointed in July last, and though he cannot alter the rules of the prison system, he has altered the spirit in which they used to be carried out under his predecessor. He is very popular with the prisoners and with the warders. Indeed he has quite elevated the whole tone of the prison-life. Upon the other hand, the system is of course beyond his reach as far as altering its rules is concerned. I have no doubt that he sees daily much of what he knows to be unjust, stupid, and cruel. But his hands are tied. Of course I have no knowledge of his real views of the case of A. 2. 11, nor, indeed, of any of his views on our present system. I merely judge him by the complete change he brought about in Reading Prison. Under his predecessor the system was carried out with the greatest harshness and stupidity.—I remain, Sir, your obedient servant,

OSCAR WILDE.

France, May 27th, 1897.

About Author

Oscar Fingal O'Flahertie Wills Wilde (16 October 1854 – 30 November 1900) was an Irish poet and playwright. After writing in different forms throughout the 1880s, the early 1890s saw him become one of the most popular playwrights in London. He is best remembered for his epigrams and plays, his novel The Picture of Dorian Gray, and the circumstances of his criminal conviction for "gross indecency", imprisonment, and early death at age 46.

Wilde's parents were successful Anglo-Irish intellectuals in Dublin. A young Wilde learned to speak fluent French and German. At university, Wilde read Greats; he demonstrated himself to be an exceptional classicist, first at Trinity College Dublin, then at Oxford. He became associated with the emerging philosophy of aestheticism, led by two of his tutors, Walter Pater and John Ruskin. After university, Wilde moved to London into fashionable cultural and social circles.

As a spokesman for aestheticism, he tried his hand at various literary activities: he published a book of poems, lectured in the United States and Canada on the new "English Renaissance in Art" and interior decoration, and then returned to London where he worked prolifically as a journalist. Known for his biting wit, flamboyant dress and glittering conversational skill, Wilde became one of the best-known personalities of his day. At the turn of the 1890s, he refined his ideas about the supremacy of art in a series of dialogues and essays, and incorporated themes of decadence, duplicity, and beauty into what would be his only novel, The Picture of Dorian Gray (1890). The opportunity to construct aesthetic details precisely, and combine them with larger social themes, drew Wilde to write drama. He wrote Salome (1891) in French while in Paris but it was refused a licence for England due to an absolute prohibition on the portrayal of Biblical subjects on the English stage. Unperturbed, Wilde produced four society comedies in the early 1890s, which made him one of the most successful playwrights of late-Victorian London.

At the height of his fame and success, while The Importance of b.. Earnest (1895) was still being performed in London, Wilde had the Marquess of Queensberry prosecuted for criminal libel. The Marquess was the father of Wilde's lover, Lord Alfred Douglas. The libel trial unearthed evidence that caused Wilde to drop his charges and led to his own arrest and trial for gross indecency with men. After two more trials he was convicted and sentenced to two years' hard labour, the maximum penalty, and was jailed from 1895 to 1897. During his last year in prison, he wrote De Profundis (published posthumously in 1905), a long letter which discusses his spiritual journey through his trials, forming a dark counterpoint to his earlier philosophy of pleasure. On his release, he left immediately for France, never to return to Ireland or Britain. There he wrote his last work, The Ballad of Reading Gaol (1898), a long poem commemorating the harsh rhythms of prison life.

Early life

Oscar Wilde was born at 21 Westland Row, Dublin (now home of the Oscar Wilde Centre, Trinity College), the second of three children born to Anglo-Irish Sir William Wilde and Jane Wilde, two years behind his brother William ("Willie"). Wilde's mother had distant Italian ancestry, and under the pseudonym "Speranza" (the Italian word for 'hope'), wrote poetry for the revolutionary Young Irelanders in 1848; she was a lifelong Irish nationalist. She read the Young Irelanders' poetry to Oscar and Willie, inculcating a love of these poets in her sons. Lady Wilde's interest in the neo-classical revival showed in the paintings and busts of ancient Greece and Rome in her home.

William Wilde was Ireland's leading oto-ophthalmologic (ear and eye) surgeon and was knighted in 1864 for his services as medical adviser and assistant commissioner to the censuses of Ireland. He also wrote books about Irish archaeology and peasant folklore. A renowned philanthropist, his dispensary for the care of the city's poor at the rear of Trinity College, Dublin, was the forerunner of the Dublin Eye and Ear Hospital, now located at Adelaide Road. On his father's side Wilde was descended from a Dutchman, Colonel de Wilde, who went to Ireland with King William of Orange's invading army in 1690, and numerous Anglo-Irish ancestors. On his mother's side, Wilde's ancestors included a bricklayer from County Durham, who emigrated to Ireland sometime in the 1770s.

Wilde was baptised as an infant in St. Mark's Church, Dublin, the local Church of Ireland (Anglican) church. When the church was closed, the records were moved to the nearby St. Ann's Church, Dawson Street. Davis Coakley mentions a second baptism by a Catholic priest, Father Prideaux Fox, who befriended Oscar's mother circa 1859. According to Fox's testimony in Donahoe's Magazine in 1905, Jane Wilde would visit his chapel in Glencree, County Wicklow, for Mass and would take her sons with her. She asked Father Fox in this period to baptise her sons.

Fox described it in this way:

> "I am not sure if she ever became a Catholic herself but it was not long before she asked me to instruct two of her children, one of them being the future erratic genius, Oscar Wilde. After a few weeks I baptized these two children, Lady Wilde herself being present on the occasion.

In addition to his children with his wife, Sir William Wilde was the father of three children born out of wedlock before his marriage: Henry Wilson, born in 1838 to one woman, and Emily and Mary Wilde, born in 1847 and 1849, respectively, to a second woman. Sir William acknowledged paternity of his illegitimate or "natural" children and provided for their education, arranging for them to be reared by his relatives rather than with his legitimate children in his family household with his wife.

In 1855, the family moved to No. 1 Merrion Square, where Wilde's sister, Isola, was born in 1857. The Wildes' new home was larger. With both his parents' success and delight in social life, the house soon became the site of a "unique medical and cultural milieu". Guests at their salon included Sheridan Le Fanu, Charles Lever, George Petrie, Isaac Butt, William Rowan Hamilton and Samuel Ferguson.

Until he was nine, Oscar Wilde was educated at home, where a French nursemaid and a German governess taught him their languages. He attended Portora Royal School in Enniskillen, County Fermanagh, from 1864 to 1871. Until his early twenties, Wilde summered at the villa, Moytura House, which his father had built in Cong, County Mayo. There the young Wilde and his brother Willie played with George Moore.

Isola died at age nine of meningitis. Wilde's poem "Requiescat" is written to her memory.

> "Tread lightly, she is near
>
> Under the snow
>
> Speak gently, she can hear
>
> the daisies grow"

University education: 1870s

Trinity College, Dublin

Wilde left Portora with a royal scholarship to read classics at Trinity College, Dublin, from 1871 to 1874, sharing rooms with his older brother Willie Wilde. Trinity, one of the leading classical schools, placed him with scholars such as R. Y. Tyrell, Arthur Palmer, Edward Dowden and his tutor, Professor J. P. Mahaffy, who inspired his interest in Greek literature. As a student Wilde worked with Mahaffy on the latter's book Social Life in Greece. Wilde, despite later reservations, called Mahaffy "my first and best teacher" and "the scholar who showed me how to love Greek things".For his part, Mahaffy boasted of having created Wilde; later, he said Wilde was "the only blot on my tutorship".

The University Philosophical Society also provided an education, as members discussed intellectual and artistic subjects such as Dante Gabriel Rossetti and Algernon Charles Swinburne weekly. Wilde quickly became an established member – the members' suggestion book for 1874 contains two pages of banter (sportingly) mocking Wilde's emergent aestheticism. He presented a paper titled "Aesthetic Morality". At Trinity, Wilde established himself as an outstanding student: he came first in his class in his first year, won a scholarship by competitive examination in his second and, in his finals, won the Berkeley Gold Medal in Greek, the University's highest academic award. He was encouraged to compete for a demyship to Magdalen College, Oxford – which he won easily, having already studied Greek for over nine years.

232

Magdalen College, Oxford

At Magdalen, he read Greats from 1874 to 1878, and from there he applied to join the Oxford Union, but failed to be elected.

Attracted by its dress, secrecy, and ritual, Wilde petitioned the Apollo Masonic Lodge at Oxford, and was soon raised to the "Sublime Degree of Master Mason".During a resurgent interest in Freemasonry in his third year, he commented he "would be awfully sorry to give it up if I secede from the Protestant Heresy". Wilde's active involvement in Freemasonry lasted only for the time he spent at Oxford; he allowed his membership of the Apollo University Lodge to lapse after failing to pay subscriptions.

Catholicism deeply appealed to him, especially its rich liturgy, and he discussed converting to it with clergy several times. In 1877, Wilde was left speechless after an audience with Pope Pius IX in Rome.He eagerly read the books of Cardinal Newman, a noted Anglican priest who had converted to Catholicism and risen in the church hierarchy. He became more serious in 1878, when he met the Reverend Sebastian Bowden, a priest in the Brompton Oratory who had received some high-profile converts. Neither his father, who threatened to cut off his funds, nor Mahaffy thought much of the plan; but mostly Wilde, the supreme individualist, balked at the last minute from pledging himself to any formal creed. On the appointed day of his baptism, Wilde sent Father Bowden a bunch of altar lilies instead. Wilde did retain a lifelong interest in Catholic theology and liturgy.

While at Magdalen College, Wilde became particularly well known for his role in the aesthetic and decadent movements. He wore his hair long, openly scorned "manly" sports though he occasionally boxed, and he decorated his rooms with peacock feathers, lilies, sunflowers, blue china and other objets d'art. He once remarked to friends, whom he entertained lavishly, "I find it harder and harder every day to live up to my blue china." The line quickly became famous, accepted as a slogan by aesthetes but used against them by critics who sensed in it a terrible vacuousness. Some elements disdained the aesthetes, but their languishing attitudes and showy costumes became a recognised pose. Wilde was once physically attacked by a group of four fellow students, and dealt with them single-handedly, surprising critics. By his third year Wilde had truly begun to develop himself and his myth, and considered his learning to be more expansive than what was within the prescribed texts. This attitude resulted in his being rusticated for one term, after he had returned late to a college term from a trip to Greece with Mahaffy.

Wilde did not meet Walter Pater until his third year, but had been enthralled by his Studies in the History of the Renaissance, published during Wilde's final year in Trinity. Pater argued that man's sensibility to beauty should be refined above all else, and that each moment should be felt to its fullest extent. Years later, in De Profundis, Wilde described Pater's Studies... as "that book that has had such a strange influence over my life".He learned tracts of the book by heart, and carried it with him on travels in later years. Pater gave Wilde his sense of almost flippant devotion to art, though he gained a purpose for it through the lectures and writings of critic John Ruskin. Ruskin despaired at the self-validating aestheticism of Pater, arguing that the importance of art lies in its potential for the betterment of society. Ruskin admired beauty, but believed it must be allied with, and applied to, moral good. When Wilde eagerly attended Ruskin's lecture series The Aesthetic and Mathematic Schools of Art in Florence, he learned about aesthetics as the non-mathematical elements of painting. Despite being given to neither early rising nor manual labour, Wilde volunteered for Ruskin's project to convert a swampy country lane into a smart road neatly edged with flowers.

Wilde won the 1878 Newdigate Prize for his poem "Ravenna", which reflected on his visit there the year before, and he duly read it at Encaenia. In November 1878, he graduated with a double first in his B.A. of Classical Moderations and Literae Humaniores (Greats). Wilde wrote to a friend, "The dons are 'astonied' beyond words – the Bad Boy doing so well in the end!"

Apprenticeship of an aesthete: 1880s

Debut in society

After graduation from Oxford, Wilde returned to Dublin, where he met again Florence Balcombe, a childhood sweetheart. She became engaged to Bram Stoker and they married in 1878. Wilde was disappointed but stoic:

he wrote to her, remembering "the two sweet years – the sweetest years of all my youth" during which they had been close. He also stated his intention to "return to England, probably for good." This he did in 1878, only briefly visiting Ireland twice after that.

Unsure of his next step, Wilde wrote to various acquaintances enquiring about Classics positions at Oxford or Cambridge. The Rise of Historical Criticism was his submission for the Chancellor's Essay prize of 1879, which, though no longer a student, he was still eligible to enter. Its subject, "Historical Criticism among the Ancients" seemed ready-made for Wilde – with both his skill in composition and ancient learning – but he struggled to find his voice with the long, flat, scholarly style. Unusually, no prize was awarded that year.

With the last of his inheritance from the sale of his father's houses, he set himself up as a bachelor in London. The 1881 British Census listed Wilde as a boarder at 1 (now 44) Tite Street, Chelsea, where Frank Miles, a society painter, was the head of the household. Wilde spent the next six years in London and Paris, and in the United States, where he travelled to deliver lectures.

He had been publishing lyrics and poems in magazines since entering Trinity College, especially in Kottabos and the Dublin University Magazine. In mid-1881, at 27 years old, he published Poems, which collected, revised and expanded his poems.

The book was generally well received, and sold out its first print run of 750 copies. Punch was less enthusiastic, saying "The poet is Wilde, but his poetry's tame". By a tight vote, the Oxford Union condemned the book for alleged plagiarism. The librarian, who had requested the book for the library, returned the presentation copy to Wilde with a note of apology. Biographer Richard Ellmann argues that Wilde's poem "Hélas!" was a sincere, though flamboyant, attempt to explain the dichotomies the poet saw in himself; one line reads: "To drift with every passion till my soul

Is a stringed lute on which all winds can play".

The book had further printings in 1882. It was bound in a rich, enamel parchment cover (embossed with gilt blossom) and printed on hand-made Dutch paper; over the next few years, Wilde presented many copies to the dignitaries and writers who received him during his lecture tours.

America: 1882

Aestheticism was sufficiently in vogue to be caricatured by Gilbert and Sullivan in Patience (1881). Richard D'Oyly Carte, an English impresario, invited Wilde to make a lecture tour of North America, simultaneously priming the pump for the US tour of Patience and selling this most charming aesthete to the American public. Wilde journeyed on the SS Arizona, arriving 2 January 1882, and disembarking the following day. Originally planned to last four months, it continued for almost a year due to the commercial success. Wilde sought to transpose the beauty he saw in art into daily life. This was a practical as well as philosophical project: in Oxford he had surrounded himself with blue china and lilies, and now one of his lectures was on interior design.

When asked to explain reports that he had paraded down Piccadilly in London carrying a lily, long hair flowing, Wilde replied, "It's not whether I did it or not that's important, but whether people believed I did it". Wilde believed that the artist should hold forth higher ideals, and that pleasure and beauty would replace utilitarian ethics.

Wilde and aestheticism were both mercilessly caricatured and criticised in the press; the Springfield Republican, for instance, commented on Wilde's behaviour during his visit to Boston to lecture on aestheticism, suggesting that Wilde's conduct was more a bid for notoriety rather than devotion to beauty and the aesthetic. T. W. Higginson, a cleric and abolitionist, wrote in "Unmanly Manhood" of his general concern that Wilde, "whose only distinction is that he has written a thin volume of very mediocre verse", would improperly influence the behaviour of men and women.

According to biographer Michèle Mendelssohn, Wilde was the subject of anti-Irish caricature and was portrayed as a monkey, a blackface performer and a Christy's Minstrel throughout his career. "Harper's Weekly put a sunflower-worshipping monkey dressed as Wilde on the front of the January 1882 issue. The magazine didn't let its reputation for quality impede its expression of what are now considered odious ethnic and racial ideologies. The drawing stimulated other American maligners and, in England, had a full-page reprint in the Lady's Pictorial. ... When the National Republican discussed Wilde, it was to explain 'a few items as to the animal's pedigree.' And on 22 January 1882 the Washington Post illustrated the Wild Man of Borneo alongside Oscar Wilde of England and asked 'How far is it from this to this?' "Though his press reception was hostile, Wilde was well received in diverse settings across America; he drank whiskey with miners in Leadville, Colorado, and was fêted at the most fashionable salons in many cities he visited.

London life and marriage

His earnings, plus expected income from The Duchess of Padua, allowed him to move to Paris between February and mid-May 1883. While there he met Robert Sherard, whom he entertained constantly. "We are dining on the Duchess tonight", Wilde would declare before taking him to an expensive restaurant. In August he briefly returned to New York for the production of Vera, his first play, after it was turned down in London. He reportedly entertained the other passengers with "Ave Imperatrix!, A Poem on England", about the rise and fall of empires. E. C. Stedman, in Victorian Poets, describes this "lyric to England" as "manly verse – a poetic and eloquent invocation". The play was initially well received by the audience, but when the critics wrote lukewarm reviews, attendance fell sharply and the play closed a week after it had opened.

Wilde had to return to England, where he continued to lecture on topics including Personal Impressions of America, The Value of Art in Modern Life, and Dress.

In London, he had been introduced in 1881 to Constance Lloyd, daughter of Horace Lloyd, a wealthy Queen's Counsel, and his wife. She happened to be visiting Dublin in 1884, when Wilde was lecturing at the Gaiety Theatre. He proposed to her, and they married on 29 May 1884 at the Anglican St James's Church, Paddington, in London. Although Constance had an annual allowance of £250, which was generous for a young woman (equivalent to about £25,600 in current value), the Wildes had relatively luxurious tastes. They had preached to others for so long on the subject of design that people expected their home to set new standards. No. 16, Tite Street was duly renovated in seven months at considerable expense. The couple had two sons together, Cyril (1885) and Vyvyan (1886). Wilde became the sole literary signatory of George Bernard Shaw's petition for a pardon of the anarchists arrested (and later executed) after the Haymarket massacre in Chicago in 1886.

Robert Ross had read Wilde's poems before they met at Oxford in 1886. He seemed unrestrained by the Victorian prohibition against homosexuality, and became estranged from his family. By Richard Ellmann's account, he was a precocious seventeen-year-old who "so young and yet so knowing, was determined to seduce Wilde". According to Daniel Mendelsohn, Wilde, who had long alluded to Greek love, was "initiated into homosexual sex" by Ross, while his "marriage had begun to unravel after his wife's second pregnancy, which left him physically repelled".

Prose writing: 1886–91

Journalism and editorship: 1886–89

Criticism over artistic matters in The Pall Mall Gazette provoked a letter in self-defence, and soon Wilde was a contributor to that and other journals during 1885–87. He enjoyed reviewing and journalism; the form suited his style. He could organise and share his views on art, literature and life, yet in a format less tedious than lecturing. Buoyed up, his reviews were largely chatty and positive. Wilde, like his parents before him, also supported the cause of Irish nationalism. When Charles Stewart Parnell was falsely accused of inciting murder, Wilde wrote a series of astute columns defending him in the Daily Chronicle.

His flair, having previously been put mainly into socialising, suited journalism and rapidly attracted notice. With his youth nearly over, and a family to support, in mid-1887 Wilde became the editor of The Lady's World magazine, his name prominently appearing on the cover. He promptly renamed it as The Woman's World and raised its tone, adding serious articles on parenting, culture, and politics, while keeping discussions of fashion and arts. Two pieces of fiction were usually included, one to be read to children, the other for the ladies themselves. Wilde worked hard to solicit good contributions from his wide artistic acquaintance, including those of Lady Wilde and his wife Constance, while his own "Literary and Other Notes" were themselves popular and amusing.

The initial vigour and excitement which he brought to the job began to fade as administration, commuting and office life became tedious. At the same time as Wilde's interest flagged, the publishers became concerned anew about circulation: sales, at the relatively high price of one shilling, remained low. Increasingly sending instructions to the magazine by letter, Wilde began a new period of creative work and his own column appeared less regularly.In October 1889, Wilde had finally found his voice in prose and, at the end of the second volume, Wilde left The Woman's World. The magazine outlasted him by one issue.

If Wilde's period at the helm of the magazine was a mixed success from an organizational point of view, it played a pivotal role in his development as a writer and facilitated his ascent to fame. Whilst Wilde the journalist supplied articles under the guidance of his editors, Wilde the editor was forced to learn to manipulate the literary marketplace on his own terms.

During the late 1880s, Wilde was a close friend of the artist James NcNeill Whistler and they dined together on many occasions. At one of these dinners, Whistler said a bon mot that Wilde found particularly witty, Wilde exclaimed that he wished that he had said it, and Whistler retorted "You will, Oscar, you will".Herbert Vivian—a mutual friend of Wilde and Whistler—attended the dinner and recorded it in his article The Reminiscences of a Short Life which appeared in The Sun in 1889. The article alleged that Wilde had a habit of passing off other people's witticisms as his own—especially Whistler's. Wilde considered Vivian's article to be a scurrilous betrayal, and it directly caused the broken friendship between Wilde and Whistler. The Reminiscences also caused great acrimony between Wilde and Vivian, Wilde accusing Vivian of "the inaccuracy of an eavesdropper with the method of a blackmailer" and banishing Vivian from his circle.

Shorter fiction

Wilde published The Happy Prince and Other Tales in 1888, and had been regularly writing fairy stories for magazines. In 1891 he published two more collections, Lord Arthur Savile's Crime and Other Stories, and in September A House of Pomegranates was dedicated "To Constance Mary Wilde". "The Portrait of Mr. W. H.", which Wilde had begun in 1887, was first published in Blackwood's Edinburgh Magazine in July 1889.It is a short story, which reports a conversation, in which the theory that Shakespeare's sonnets were written out of the poet's love of the boy actor "Willie Hughes", is advanced, retracted, and then propounded again. The only evidence for this is two supposed puns within the sonnets themselves.

The anonymous narrator is at first sceptical, then believing, finally flirtatious with the reader: he concludes that "there is really a great deal to be said of the Willie Hughes theory of Shakespeare's sonnets." By the end fact and fiction have melded together.Arthur Ransome wrote that Wilde "read something of himself into Shakespeare's sonnets" and became fascinated with the "Willie Hughes theory" despite the lack of biographical evidence for the historical William Hughes' existence. Instead of writing a short but serious essay on the question, Wilde tossed the theory amongst the three characters of the story, allowing it to unfold as background to the plot. The story thus is an early masterpiece of Wilde's combining many elements that interested him: conversation, literature and the idea that to shed oneself of an idea one must first convince another of its truth.Ransome concludes that Wilde succeeds precisely because the literary criticism is unveiled with such a deft touch.

Though containing nothing but "special pleading", it would not, he says "be possible to build an airier castle in Spain than this of the imaginary William Hughes" we continue listening nonetheless to be charmed by the telling. "You must believe in Willie Hughes," Wilde told an acquaintance, "I almost do, myself."

Essays and dialogues

Wilde, having tired of journalism, had been busy setting out his aesthetic ideas more fully in a series of longer prose pieces which were published in the major literary-intellectual journals of the day. In January 1889, The Decay of Lying: A Dialogue appeared in The Nineteenth Century, and Pen, Pencil and Poison, a satirical biography of Thomas Griffiths Wainewright, in The Fortnightly Review, edited by Wilde's friend Frank Harris. Two of Wilde's four writings on aesthetics are dialogues: though Wilde had evolved professionally from lecturer to writer, he retained an oral tradition of sorts. Having always excelled as a wit and raconteur, he often composed by assembling phrases, bons mots and witticisms into a longer, cohesive work.

Wilde was concerned about the effect of moralising on art; he believed in art's redemptive, developmental powers: "Art is individualism, and individualism is a disturbing and disintegrating force. There lies its immense value. For what it seeks is to disturb monotony of type, slavery of custom, tyranny of habit, and the reduction of man to the level of a machine." In his only political text, The Soul of Man Under Socialism, he argued political conditions should establish this primacy – private property should be abolished, and cooperation should be substituted for competition. At the same time, he stressed that the government most amenable to artists was no government at all. Wilde envisioned a society where mechanisation has freed human effort from the burden of necessity, effort which can instead be expended on artistic creation. George Orwell summarised, "In effect, the world will be populated by artists, each striving after perfection in the way that seems best to him."

This point of view did not align him with the Fabians, intellectual socialists who advocated using state apparatus to change social conditions, nor did it endear him to the monied classes whom he had previously entertained. Hesketh Pearson, introducing a collection of Wilde's essays in 1950, remarked how The Soul of Man Under Socialism had been an inspirational text for revolutionaries in Tsarist Russia but laments that in the Stalinist era "it is doubtful whether there are any uninspected places in which it could now be hidden".

Wilde considered including this pamphlet and The Portrait of Mr. W.H., his essay-story on Shakespeare's sonnets, in a new anthology in 1891, but eventually decided to limit it to purely aesthetic subjects. Intentions packaged revisions of four essays: The Decay of Lying, Pen, Pencil and Poison, The Truth of Masks (first published 1885), and The Critic as Artist in two parts. For Pearson the biographer, the essays and dialogues exhibit every aspect of Wilde's genius and character: wit, romancer, talker, lecturer, humanist and scholar and concludes that "no other productions of his have as varied an appeal". 1891 turned out to be Wilde's annus mirabilis; apart from his three collections he also produced his only novel.

The Picture of Dorian Gray

The first version of The Picture of Dorian Gray was published as the lead story in the July 1890 edition of Lippincott's Monthly Magazine, along with five others. The story begins with a man painting a picture of Gray. When Gray, who has a "face like ivory and rose leaves", sees his finished portrait, he breaks down. Distraught that his beauty will fade while the portrait stays beautiful, he inadvertently makes a Faustian bargain in which only the painted image grows old while he stays beautiful and young. For Wilde, the purpose of art would be to guide life as if beauty alone were its object. As Gray's portrait allows him to escape the corporeal ravages of his hedonism, Wilde sought to juxtapose the beauty he saw in art with daily life.

Reviewers immediately criticised the novel's decadence and homosexual allusions; The Daily Chronicle for example, called it "unclean", "poisonous", and "heavy with the mephitic odours of moral and spiritual putrefaction". Which he clarified his stance on ethics and aesthetics in art – "If a work of art is rich and vital and complete, those who have artistic instincts will see its beauty and those to whom ethics appeal more strongly will see its moral lesson." He nevertheless revised it extensively for book publication in 1891: six new chapters were added, some overtly decadent passages and homo-eroticism excised, and a preface was included consisting of twenty two epigrams, such as "Books are well written, or badly written. That is all."

Contemporary reviewers and modern critics have postulated numerous possible sources of the story, a search Jershua McCormack argues is futile because Wilde "has tapped a root of Western folklore so deep and ubiquitous that the story has escaped its origins and returned to the oral tradition." Wilde claimed the plot was "an idea that is as old as the history of literature but to which I have given a new form".Modern critic Robin McKie considered the novel to be technically mediocre, saying that the conceit of the plot had guaranteed its fame, but the device is never pushed to its full.On the other hand, Robert McCrum of The Guardian deemed it the 27th best novel ever written in English, calling it "an arresting, and slightly camp, exercise in late-Victorian gothic."

Theatrical career: 1892–95

Salomé

The 1891 census records the Wildes' residence at 16 Tite Street, where he lived with his wife Constance and two sons. Wilde though, not content with being better known than ever in London, returned to Paris in October 1891, this time as a respected writer. He was received at the salons littéraires, including the famous mardis of Stéphane Mallarmé, a renowned symbolist poet of the time. Wilde's two plays during the 1880s, Vera; or, The Nihilists and The Duchess of Padua, had not met with much success. He had continued his interest in the theatre and now, after finding his voice in prose, his thoughts turned again to the dramatic form as the biblical iconography of Salome filled his mind. One evening, after discussing depictions of Salome throughout history, he returned to his hotel and noticed a blank copybook lying on the desk, and it occurred to him to write in it what he had been saying. The result was a new play, Salomé, written rapidly and in French.

A tragedy, it tells the story of Salome, the stepdaughter of the tetrarch Herod Antipas, who, to her stepfather's dismay but mother's delight, requests the head of Jokanaan (John the Baptist) on a silver platter as a reward for dancing the Dance of the Seven Veils. When Wilde returned to London just before Christmas the Paris Echo referred to him as "le great event" of the season. Rehearsals of the play, starring Sarah Bernhardt, began but the play was refused a licence by the Lord Chamberlain, since it depicted biblical characters. Salome was published jointly in Paris and London in 1893, but was not performed until 1896 in Paris, during Wilde's later incarceration.

Comedies of society

Wilde, who had first set out to irritate Victorian society with his dress and talking points, then outrage it with Dorian Gray, his novel of vice hidden beneath art, finally found a way to critique society on its own terms. Lady Windermere's Fan was first performed on 20 February 1892 at St James's Theatre, packed with the cream of society. On the surface a witty comedy, there is subtle subversion underneath: "it concludes with collusive concealment rather than collective disclosure". The audience, like Lady Windermere, are forced to soften harsh social codes in favour of a more nuanced view. The play was enormously popular, touring the country for months, but largely trashed by conservative critics. It was followed by A Woman of No Importance in 1893, another Victorian comedy, revolving around the spectre of illegitimate births, mistaken identities and late revelations. Wilde was commissioned to write two more plays and An Ideal Husband, written in 1894, followed in January 1895.

Peter Raby said these essentially English plays were well-pitched, "Wilde, with one eye on the dramatic genius of Ibsen, and the other on the commercial competition in London's West End, targeted his audience with adroit precision".

Queensberry family

In mid-1891 Lionel Johnson introduced Wilde to Lord Alfred Douglas, Johnson's cousin and an undergraduate at Oxford at the time. Known to his family and friends as "Bosie", he was a handsome and spoilt young man. An intimate friendship sprang up between Wilde and Douglas and by 1893 Wilde was infatuated with Douglas and they consorted together regularly in a tempestuous affair. If Wilde was relatively indiscreet, even flamboyant, in the way he acted, Douglas was reckless in public. Wilde, who was earning up to £100 a week from his plays (his salary at The Woman's World had been £6), indulged Douglas's every whim: material, artistic or sexual.

Douglas soon initiated Wilde into the Victorian underground of gay prostitution and Wilde was introduced to a series of young working-class male prostitutes from 1892 onwards by Alfred Taylor. These infrequent rendezvous usually took the same form: Wilde would meet the boy, offer him gifts, dine him privately and then take him to a hotel room. Unlike Wilde's idealised relations with Ross, John Gray, and Douglas, all of whom remained part of his aesthetic circle, these consorts were uneducated and knew nothing of literature. Soon his public and private lives had become sharply divided; in De Profundis he wrote to Douglas that "It was like feasting with panthers; the danger was half the excitement... I did not know that when they were to strike at me it was to be at another's piping and at another's pay."

Douglas and some Oxford friends founded a journal, The Chameleon, to which Wilde "sent a page of paradoxes originally destined for the Saturday Review". "Phrases and Philosophies for the Use of the Young" was to come under attack six months later at Wilde's trial, where he was forced to defend the magazine to which he had sent his work.In any case, it became unique: The Chameleon was not published again.

Lord Alfred's father, the Marquess of Queensberry, was known for his outspoken atheism, brutish manner and creation of the modern rules of boxing. Queensberry, who feuded regularly with his son, confronted Wilde and Lord Alfred about the nature of their relationship several times, but Wilde was able to mollify him. In June 1894, he called on Wilde at 16 Tite Street, without an appointment, and clarified his stance: "I do not say that you are it, but you look it, and pose at it, which is just as bad. And if I catch you and my son again in any public restaurant I will thrash you" to which Wilde responded: "I don't know what the Queensberry rules are, but the Oscar Wilde rule is to shoot on sight".His account in De Profundis was less triumphant: "It was when, in my library at Tite Street, waving his small hands in the air in epileptic fury, your father... stood uttering every foul word his foul mind could think of, and screaming the loathsome threats he afterwards with such cunning carried out". Queensberry only described the scene once, saying Wilde had "shown him the white feather", meaning he had acted in a cowardly way. Though trying to remain calm, Wilde saw that he was becoming ensnared in a brutal family quarrel. He did not wish to bear Queensberry's insults, but he knew to confront him could lead to disaster were his liaisons disclosed publicly.

The Importance of Being Earnest

Wilde's final play again returns to the theme of switched identities: the play's two protagonists engage in "bunburying" (the maintenance of alternative personas in the town and country) which allows them to escape Victorian social mores.Earnest is even lighter in tone than Wilde's earlier comedies. While their characters often rise to serious themes in moments of crisis, Earnest lacks the by-now stock Wildean characters: there is no "woman with a past", the principals are neither villainous nor cunning, simply idle cultivés, and the idealistic young women are not that innocent. Mostly set in drawing rooms and almost completely lacking in action or violence, Earnest lacks the self-conscious decadence found in The Picture of Dorian Gray and Salome.

The play, now considered Wilde's masterpiece, was rapidly written in Wilde's artistic maturity in late 1894. It was first performed on 14 February 1895, at St James's Theatre in London, Wilde's second collaboration with George Alexander, the actor-manager. Both author and producer assiduously revised, prepared and rehearsed every line, scene and setting in the months before the premiere, creating a carefully constructed representation of late-Victorian society, yet simultaneously mocking it. During rehearsal Alexander requested that Wilde shorten the play from four acts to three, which the author did. Premieres at St James's seemed like "brilliant parties", and the opening of The Importance of Being Earnest was no exception. Allan Aynesworth (who played Algernon) recalled to Hesketh Pearson, "In my fifty-three years of acting, I never remember a greater triumph than [that] first night."Earnest's immediate reception as Wilde's best work to date finally crystallised his fame into a solid artistic reputation. The Importance of Being Earnest remains his most popular play.

Wilde's professional success was mirrored by an escalation in his feud with Queensberry. Queensberry had planned to insult Wilde publicly by throwing a bouquet of rotting vegetables onto the stage; Wilde was tipped off and had Queensberry barred from entering the theatre.Fifteen weeks later Wilde was in prison.

Trials

246

Wilde v. Queensberry

On 18 February 1895, the Marquess left his calling card at Wilde's club, the Albemarle, inscribed: "For Oscar Wilde, posing somdomite" Wilde, encouraged by Douglas and against the advice of his friends, initiated a private prosecution against Queensberry for libel, since the note amounted to a public accusation that Wilde had committed the crime of sodomy.

Queensberry was arrested for criminal libel; a charge carrying a possible sentence of up to two years in prison. Under the 1843 Libel Act, Queensberry could avoid conviction for libel only by demonstrating that his accusation was in fact true, and furthermore that there was some "public benefit" to having made the accusation openly. Queensberry's lawyers thus hired private detectives to find evidence of Wilde's homosexual liaisons.

Wilde's friends had advised him against the prosecution at a Saturday Review meeting at the Café Royal on 24 March 1895; Frank Harris warned him that "they are going to prove sodomy against you" and advised him to flee to France. Wilde and Douglas walked out in a huff, Wilde saying "it is at such moments as these that one sees who are one's true friends". The scene was witnessed by George Bernard Shaw who recalled it to Arthur Ransome a day or so before Ransome's trial for libelling Douglas in 1913. To Ransome it confirmed what he had said in his 1912 book on Wilde; that Douglas's rivalry for Wilde with Robbie Ross and his arguments with his father had resulted in Wilde's public disaster; as Wilde wrote in De Profundis. Douglas lost his case. Shaw included an account of the argument between Harris, Douglas and Wilde in the preface to his play The Dark Lady of the Sonnets.

The libel trial became a cause célèbre as salacious details of Wilde's private life with Taylor and Douglas began to appear in the press. A team of private detectives had directed Queensberry's lawyers, led by Edward Carson QC, to the world of the Victorian underground. Wilde's association with blackmailers and male prostitutes, cross-dressers and homosexual brothels was recorded, and various persons involved were interviewed, some being coerced to appear as witnesses since they too were accomplices to the crimes of which Wilde was accused.

The trial opened on 3 April 1895 before Justice Richard Henn Collins amid scenes of near hysteria both in the press and the public galleries. The extent of the evidence massed against Wilde forced him to declare meekly, "I am the prosecutor in this case" Wilde's lawyer, Sir Edward George Clarke, opened the case by pre-emptively asking Wilde about two suggestive letters Wilde had written to Douglas, which the defence had in its possession. He characterised the first as a "prose sonnet" and admitted that the "poetical language" might seem strange to the court but claimed its intent was innocent. Wilde stated that the letters had been obtained by blackmailers who had attempted to extort money from him, but he had refused, suggesting they should take the £60 (equal to £6,800 today) offered, "unusual for a prose piece of that length". He claimed to regard the letters as works of art rather than something of which to be ashamed.

Carson, a fellow Dubliner who had attended Trinity College, Dublin at the same time as Wilde, cross-examined Wilde on how he perceived the moral content of his works. Wilde replied with characteristic wit and flippancy, claiming that works of art are not capable of being moral or immoral but only well or poorly made, and that only "brutes and illiterates", whose views on art "are incalculably stupid", would make such judgements about art. Carson, a leading barrister, diverged from the normal practice of asking closed questions. Carson pressed Wilde on each topic from every angle, squeezing out nuances of meaning from Wilde's answers, removing them from their aesthetic context and portraying Wilde as evasive and decadent. While Wilde won the most laughs from the court, Carson scored the most legal points. To undermine Wilde's credibility, and to justify Queensberry's description of Wilde as a "posing somdomite", Carson drew from the witness an admission of his capacity for "posing", by demonstrating that he had lied about his age on oath. Playing on this, he returned to the topic throughout his cross-examination. Carson also tried to justify Queensberry's characterisation by quoting from Wilde's novel, The Picture of Dorian Gray, referring in particular to a scene in the second chapter, in which Lord Henry Wotton explains his decadent philosophy to Dorian, an "innocent young man", in Carson's words.

248

Carson then moved to the factual evidence and questioned Wilde about his friendships with younger, lower-class men. Wilde admitted being on a first-name basis and lavishing gifts upon them, but insisted that nothing untoward had occurred and that the men were merely good friends of his. Carson repeatedly pointed out the unusual nature of these relationships and insinuated that the men were prostitutes. Wilde replied that he did not believe in social barriers, and simply enjoyed the society of young men. Then Carson asked Wilde directly whether he had ever kissed a certain servant boy, Wilde responded, "Oh, dear no. He was a particularly plain boy – unfortunately ugly – I pitied him for it." Carson pressed him on the answer, repeatedly asking why the boy's ugliness was relevant. Wilde hesitated, then for the first time became flustered: "You sting me and insult me and try to unnerve me; and at times one says things flippantly when one ought to speak more seriously."

In his opening speech for the defence, Carson announced that he had located several male prostitutes who were to testify that they had had sex with Wilde. On the advice of his lawyers, Wilde dropped the prosecution. Queensberry was found not guilty, as the court declared that his accusation that Wilde was "posing as a Somdomite " was justified, "true in substance and in fact".Under the Libel Act 1843, Queensberry's acquittal rendered Wilde legally liable for the considerable expenses Queensberry had incurred in his defence, which left Wilde bankrupt.

Regina v. Wilde

After Wilde left the court, a warrant for his arrest was applied for on charges of sodomy and gross indecency. Robbie Ross found Wilde at the Cadogan Hotel, Pont Street, Knightsbridge, with Reginald Turner; both men advised Wilde to go at once to Dover and try to get a boat to France; his mother advised him to stay and fight. Wilde, lapsing into inaction, could only say, "The train has gone. It's too late."On 6 April 1895, Wilde was arrested for "gross indecency" under Section 11 of the Criminal Law Amendment Act 1885, a term meaning homosexual acts not amounting to buggery (an offence under a separate statute). At Wilde's instruction, Ross and Wilde's butler forced their way into the bedroom and library of 16 Tite Street, packing some personal effects, manuscripts, and letters. Wilde was then imprisoned on remand at Holloway, where he received daily visits from Douglas.

Events moved quickly and his prosecution opened on 26 April 1895, before Mr Justice Charles. Wilde pleaded not guilty. He had already begged Douglas to leave London for Paris, but Douglas complained bitterly, even wanting to give evidence; he was pressed to go and soon fled to the Hotel du Monde. Fearing persecution, Ross and many others also left the United Kingdom during this time. Under cross examination Wilde was at first hesitant, then spoke eloquently:

Charles Gill (prosecuting): What is "the love that dare not speak its name"?

Wilde: "The love that dare not speak its name" in this century is such a great affection of an elder for a younger man as there was between David and Jonathan, such as Plato made the very basis of his philosophy, and such as you find in the sonnets of Michelangelo and Shakespeare. It is that deep spiritual affection that is as pure as it is perfect. It dictates and pervades great works of art, like those of Shakespeare and Michelangelo, and those two letters of mine, such as they are. It is in this century misunderstood, so much misunderstood that it may be described as "the love that dare not speak its name", and on that account of it I am placed where I am now. It is beautiful, it is fine, it is the noblest form of affection. There is nothing unnatural about it. It is intellectual, and it repeatedly exists between an older and a younger man, when the older man has intellect, and the younger man has all the joy, hope and glamour of life before him. That it should be so, the world does not understand. The world mocks at it, and sometimes puts one in the pillory for it.

This response was counter-productive in a legal sense as it only served to reinforce the charges of homosexual behaviour.

The trial ended with the jury unable to reach a verdict. Wilde's counsel, Sir Edward Clarke, was finally able to get a magistrate to allow Wilde and his friends to post bail. The Reverend Stewart Headlam put up most of the £5,000 surety required by the court, having disagreed with Wilde's treatment by the press and the courts. Wilde was freed from Holloway and, shunning

250

attention, went into hiding at the house of Ernest and Ada Leverson, two of his firm friends. Edward Carson approached Frank Lockwood QC, the Solicitor General and asked "Can we not let up on the fellow now?" Lockwood answered that he would like to do so, but feared that the case had become too politicised to be dropped.

The final trial was presided over by Mr Justice Wills. On 25 May 1895 Wilde and Alfred Taylor were convicted of gross indecency and sentenced to two years' hard labour. The judge described the sentence, the maximum allowed, as "totally inadequate for a case such as this", and that the case was "the worst case I have ever tried". Wilde's response "And I? May I say nothing, my Lord?" was drowned out in cries of "Shame" in the courtroom.

Imprisonment

When first I was put into prison some people advised me to try and forget who I was. It was ruinous advice. It is only by realising what I am that I have found comfort of any kind. Now I am advised by others to try on my release to forget that I have ever been in a prison at all. I know that would be equally fatal. It would mean that I would always be haunted by an intolerable sense of disgrace, and that those things that are meant for me as much as for anybody else – the beauty of the sun and moon, the pageant of the seasons, the music of daybreak and the silence of great nights, the rain falling through the leaves, or the dew creeping over the grass and making it silver – would all be tainted for me, and lose their healing power, and their power of communicating joy. To regret one's own experiences is to arrest one's own development. To deny one's own experiences is to put a lie into the lips of one's own life. It is no less than a denial of the soul.

De Profundis

Wilde was incarcerated from 25 May 1895 to 18 May 1897.

He first entered Newgate Prison in London for processing, then was moved to Pentonville Prison, where the "hard labour" to which he had been sentenced consisted of many hours of walking a treadmill and picking oakum (separating the fibres in scraps of old navy ropes), and where prisoners were allowed to read only the Bible and The Pilgrim's Progress.

A few months later he was moved to Wandsworth Prison in London. Inmates there also followed the regimen of "hard labour, hard fare and a hard bed", which wore harshly on Wilde's delicate health. In November he collapsed during chapel from illness and hunger. His right ear drum was ruptured in the fall, an injury that later contributed to his death. He spent two months in the infirmary.

Richard B. Haldane, the Liberal MP and reformer, visited Wilde and had him transferred in November to Reading Gaol, 30 miles (48 km) west of London on 23 November 1895. The transfer itself was the lowest point of his incarceration, as a crowd jeered and spat at him on the railway platform. He spent the remainder of his sentence there, addressed and identified only as "C33" – the occupant of the third cell on the third floor of C ward.

About five months after Wilde arrived at Reading Gaol, Charles Thomas Wooldridge, a trooper in the Royal Horse Guards, was brought to Reading to await his trial for murdering his wife on 29 March 1896; on 17 June Wooldridge was sentenced to death and returned to Reading for his execution, which took place on Tuesday, 7 July 1896 – the first hanging at Reading in 18 years. From Wooldridge's hanging, Wilde later wrote The Ballad of Reading Gaol.

Wilde was not, at first, even allowed paper and pen but Haldane eventually succeeded in allowing access to books and writing materials. Wilde requested, among others: the Bible in French; Italian and German grammars; some Ancient Greek texts, Dante's Divine Comedy, Joris-Karl Huysmans's new French novel about Christian redemption En route, and essays by St Augustine, Cardinal Newman and Walter Pater.

Between January and March 1897 Wilde wrote a 50,000-word letter to Douglas. He was not allowed to send it, but was permitted to take it with him when released from prison. In reflective mode, Wilde coldly examines his career to date, how he had been a colourful agent provocateur in Victorian society, his art, like his paradoxes, seeking to subvert as well as sparkle. His own estimation of himself was: one who "stood in symbolic relations to the art and culture of my age". It was from these heights that his life with Douglas began, and Wilde examines that particularly closely, repudiating him for what Wilde finally sees as his arrogance and vanity: he had not forgotten Douglas' remark, when he was ill, "When you are not on your pedestal you are not interesting." Wilde blamed himself, though, for the ethical degradation of character that he allowed Douglas to bring about in him and took responsibility for his own fall, "I am here for having tried to put your father in prison." The first half concludes with Wilde forgiving Douglas, for his own sake as much as Douglas's. The second half of the letter traces Wilde's spiritual journey of redemption and fulfilment through his prison reading. He realised that his ordeal had filled his soul with the fruit of experience, however bitter it tasted at the time.

> ... I wanted to eat of the fruit of all the trees in the garden of the world ... And so, indeed, I went out, and so I lived. My only mistake was that I confined myself so exclusively to the trees of what seemed to me the sun-lit side of the garden, and shunned the other side for its shadow and its gloom.

Wilde was released from prison on 19 May 1897 and sailed that evening for Dieppe, France. He never returned to the UK.

On his release, he gave the manuscript to Ross, who may or may not have carried out Wilde's instructions to send a copy to Douglas (who later denied having received it). The letter was partially published in 1905 as De Profundis; its complete and correct publication first occurred in 1962 in The Letters of Oscar Wilde.

Decline: 1897–1900

Exile

Though Wilde's health had suffered greatly from the harshness and diet of prison, he had a feeling of spiritual renewal. He immediately wrote to the Society of Jesus requesting a six-month Catholic retreat; when the request was denied, Wilde wept. "I intend to be received into the Catholic Church before long", Wilde told a journalist who asked about his religious intentions.

He spent his last three years impoverished and in exile. He took the name "Sebastian Melmoth", after Saint Sebastian and the titular character of Melmoth the Wanderer (a Gothic novel by Charles Maturin, Wilde's great-uncle).Wilde wrote two long letters to the editor of the Daily Chronicle, describing the brutal conditions of English prisons and advocating penal reform. His discussion of the dismissal of Warder Martin for giving biscuits to an anaemic child prisoner repeated the themes of the corruption and degeneration of punishment that he had earlier outlined in The Soul of Man under Socialism.

Wilde spent mid-1897 with Robert Ross in the seaside village of Berneval-le-Grand in northern France, where he wrote The Ballad of Reading Gaol, narrating the execution of Charles Thomas Wooldridge, who murdered his wife in a rage at her infidelity. It moves from an objective story-telling to symbolic identification with the prisoners. No attempt is made to assess the justice of the laws which convicted them but rather the poem highlights the brutalisation of the punishment that all convicts share. Wilde juxtaposes the executed man and himself with the line "Yet each man kills the thing he loves". He adopted the proletarian ballad form and the author was credited as "C33", Wilde's cell number in Reading Gaol. He suggested that it be published in Reynolds' Magazine, "because it circulates widely among the criminal classes – to which I now belong – for once I will be read by my peers – a new experience for me". It was an immediate roaring commercial success, going through seven editions in less than two years, only after which "[Oscar]" was added to the title page, though many in literary circles had known Wilde to be the author. It brought him a small amount of money.

Although Douglas had been the cause of his misfortunes, he and Wilde were reunited in August 1897 at Rouen. This meeting was disapproved of by the friends and families of both men. Constance Wilde was already refusing to meet Wilde or allow him to see their sons, though she sent him money – three pounds a week. During the latter part of 1897, Wilde and Douglas lived together near Naples for a few months until they were separated by their families under the threat of cutting off all funds.

254

Wilde's final address was at the dingy Hôtel d'Alsace (now known as L'Hôtel), on rue des Beaux-Arts in Saint-Germain-des-Prés, Paris. "This poverty really breaks one's heart: it is so sale , so utterly depressing, so hopeless. Pray do what you can" he wrote to his publisher.He corrected and published An Ideal Husband and The Importance of Being Earnest, the proofs of which, according to Ellmann, show a man "very much in command of himself and of the play" but he refused to write anything else: "I can write, but have lost the joy of writing".

He wandered the boulevards alone and spent what little money he had on alcohol. A series of embarrassing chance encounters with hostile English visitors, or Frenchmen he had known in better days, drowned his spirit. Soon Wilde was sufficiently confined to his hotel to joke, on one of his final trips outside, "My wallpaper and I are fighting a duel to the death. One of us has got to go". On 12 October 1900 he sent a telegram to Ross: "Terribly weak. Please come". His moods fluctuated; Max Beerbohm relates how their mutual friend Reginald 'Reggie' Turner had found Wilde very depressed after a nightmare. "I dreamt that I had died, and was supping with the dead!" "I am sure", Turner replied, "that you must have been the life and soul of the party."Turner was one of the few of the old circle who remained with Wilde to the end and was at his bedside when he died.

Death

By 25 November 1900 Wilde had developed meningitis, then called "cerebral meningitis". Robbie Ross arrived on 29 November, sent for a priest, and Wilde was conditionally baptised into the Catholic Church by Fr Cuthbert Dunne, a Passionist priest from Dublin, Wilde having been baptised in the Church of Ireland and having moreover a recollection of Catholic baptism as a child, a fact later attested to by the minister of the sacrament, Fr Lawrence Fox.Fr Dunne recorded the baptism,

As the voiture rolled through the dark streets that wintry night, the sad story of Oscar Wilde was in part repeated to me... Robert Ross knelt by the bedside, assisting me as best he could while I administered conditional baptism, and afterwards answering the responses while I gave Extreme Unction to the prostrate man and recited the prayers for the dying. As the man was in a semi-comatose condition, I did not venture to administer the Holy Viaticum; still I must add that he could be roused and was roused from this state in my presence. When roused, he gave signs of being inwardly conscious... Indeed I was fully satisfied that he understood me when told that I was about to receive him into the Catholic Church and gave him the Last Sacraments... And when I repeated close to his ear the Holy Names, the Acts of Contrition, Faith, Hope and Charity, with acts of humble resignation to the Will of God, he tried all through to say the words after me.

Wilde died of meningitis on 30 November 1900. Different opinions are given as to the cause of the disease: Richard Ellmann claimed it was syphilitic; Merlin Holland, Wilde's grandson, thought this to be a misconception, noting that Wilde's meningitis followed a surgical intervention, perhaps a mastoidectomy; Wilde's physicians, Dr Paul Cleiss and A'Court Tucker, reported that the condition stemmed from an old suppuration of the right ear (from the prison injury, see above) treated for several years (une ancienne suppuration de l'oreille droite d'ailleurs en traitement depuis plusieurs années) and made no allusion to syphilis.

Burial

Wilde was initially buried in the Cimetière de Bagneux outside Paris; in 1909 his remains were disinterred and transferred to Père Lachaise Cemetery, inside the city. His tomb there was designed by Sir Jacob Epstein. It was commissioned by Robert Ross, who asked for a small compartment to be made for his own ashes, which were duly transferred in 1950. The modernist angel depicted as a relief on the tomb was originally complete with male genitalia, which were initially censored by French Authorities with a golden leaf. The genitals have since been vandalised; their current whereabouts are unknown. In 2000, Leon Johnson, a multimedia artist, installed a silver prosthesis to replace them. In 2011, the tomb was cleaned of the many lipstick marks left there by admirers and a glass barrier was installed to prevent further marks or damage.

The epitaph is a verse from The Ballad of Reading Gaol,

And alien tears will fill for him

Pity's long-broken urn,

For his mourners will be outcast men,

And outcasts always mourn.

Posthumous pardon

In 2017, Wilde was among an estimated 50,000 men who were pardoned for homosexual acts that were no longer considered offences under the Policing and Crime Act 2017. The Act is known informally as the Alan Turing law.

Honours

In 2014 Wilde was one of the inaugural honorees in the Rainbow Honor Walk, a walk of fame in San Francisco's Castro neighbourhood noting LGBTQ people who have "made significant contributions in their fields."

Biographies

Wilde's life has been the subject of numerous biographies since his death. The earliest were memoirs by those who knew him: often they are personal or impressionistic accounts which can be good character sketches, but are sometimes factually unreliable. Frank Harris, his friend and editor, wrote a biography, Oscar Wilde: His Life and Confessions (1916); though prone to exaggeration and sometimes factually inaccurate, it offers a good literary portrait of Wilde. Lord Alfred Douglas wrote two books about his relationship with Wilde. Oscar Wilde and Myself (1914), largely ghost-written by T. W. H. Crosland, vindictively reacted to Douglas's discovery that De Profundis was addressed to him and defensively tried to distance him from Wilde's scandalous reputation. Both authors later regretted their work. Later, in Oscar Wilde: A Summing Up (1939) and his Autobiography he was more sympathetic to Wilde. Of Wilde's other close friends, Robert Sherard; Robert Ross, his literary executor; and Charles Ricketts variously published biographies, reminiscences or correspondence. The first more or less objective biography of Wilde came about when Hesketh Pearson wrote Oscar Wilde: His Life and Wit (1946). In 1954 Wilde's son Vyvyan Holland published his memoir Son of Oscar Wilde, which recounts the difficulties Wilde's wife and children faced after his imprisonment. It was revised and updated by Merlin Holland in 1989.

Oscar Wilde, a critical study by Arthur Ransome was published in 1912. The book only briefly mentioned Wilde's life, but subsequently Ransome (and The Times Book Club) were sued for libel by Lord Alfred Douglas. In April 1913 Douglas lost the libel action after a reading of De Profundis refuted his claims.

Richard Ellmann wrote his 1987 biography Oscar Wilde, for which he posthumously won a National (USA) Book Critics Circle Award in 1988and a Pulitzer Prize in 1989. The book was the basis for the 1997 film Wilde, directed by Brian Gilbert and starring Stephen Fry as the title character.

Neil McKenna's 2003 biography, The Secret Life of Oscar Wilde, offers an exploration of Wilde's sexuality. Often speculative in nature, it was widely criticised for its pure conjecture and lack of scholarly rigour. Thomas Wright's Oscar's Books (2008) explores Wilde's reading from his childhood in Dublin to his death in Paris. After tracking down many books that once belonged to Wilde's Tite Street library (dispersed at the time of his trials), Wright was the first to examine Wilde's marginalia.

> Later on, I think everyone will recognise his achievements; his plays and essays will endure. Of course, you may think with others that his personality and conversation were far more wonderful than anything he wrote, so that his written works give only a pale reflection of his power. Perhaps that is so, and of course, it will be impossible to reproduce what is gone forever.

Robert Ross, 23 December 1900

In 2018, Matthew Sturgis' "Oscar: A Life," was published in London. The book incorporates rediscovered letters and other documents and is the most extensively researched biography of Wilde to appear since 1988.

Parisian literati, also produced several biographies and monographs on him. André Gide wrote In Memoriam, Oscar Wilde and Wilde also features in his journals. Thomas Louis, who had earlier translated books on Wilde into French, produced his own L'esprit d'Oscar Wilde in 1920. Modern books include Philippe Jullian's Oscar Wilde, and L'affaire Oscar Wilde, ou, Du danger de laisser la justice mettre le nez dans nos draps (The Oscar Wilde Affair, or, On the Danger of Allowing Justice to put its Nose in our Sheets) by Odon Vallet, a French religious historian. (Source: Wikipedia)

NOTABLE WORKS

ESSAYS

"The Decay of Lying" First published in Nineteenth Century (1889), republished in Intentions (1891).

"Pen, Pencil and Poison" First published in the Fortnightly Review (1889), republished in Intentions (1891).

"The Soul of Man under Socialism" First published in the Fortnightly Review (1891), republished in The Soul of Man (1895), privately printed.

Intentions (1891) Wilde revised his dialogues on aesthetic subjects for publication in this volume, which comprises:

- "The Critic as Artist"
- "The Decay of Lying"
- "Pen, Pencil and Poison"
- "The Truth of Masks"

"Phrases and Philosophies for the Use of the Young" first published in the Oxford student magazine The Chameleon, December 1894)

"A Few Maxims For The Instruction Of The Over-Educated" First published, anonymously, in the 1894 November 17 issue of Saturday Review.

FICTION

Novel

The Picture of Dorian Gray (1890/1891). The first version of "The Picture of Dorian Gray" was published, in a form highly edited by the magazine, as the lead story in the July 1890 edition of Lippincott's Monthly Magazine. Wilde published the longer and revised version in book form in 1891, with an added preface.

Stories

"The Portrait of Mr. W. H." (1889)

The Happy Prince and Other Tales (1888, a collection of fairy tales) consisting of:

- "The Happy Prince"
- "The Nightingale and the Rose"
- "The Selfish Giant"
- "The Devoted Friend"
- "The Remarkable Rocket"

A House of Pomegranates (1891, fairy tales)

Lord Arthur Savile's Crime and Other Stories (1891) Including "The Canterville Ghost" first published in periodical form in 1887.

Complete Short Fiction. Penguin Classics, 2003. Edited with an Introduction and Notes by Ian Small. Contains all works listed above plus Poems in Prose (1894) and one very short 'Elder-tree' (fragment).

POEMS

Ravenna (1878) Winner of the Newdigate Prize.

Poems (1881) Wilde's collection of poetry and first publication.

The Sphinx (1894)

Poems in Prose (1894)

The Ballad of Reading Gaol (1898)

PLAYS

Vera; or, The Nihilists (1880)

The Duchess of Padua (1883)

Lady Windermere's Fan (1892)

A Woman of No Importance (1893)

Salomé (French version) (1893, first performed in Paris 1896)

Salomé: A Tragedy in One Act: Translated from the French of Oscar Wilde by Lord Alfred Douglas, illustrated by Aubrey Beardsley (1894)

An Ideal Husband (1895) (text)

The Importance of Being Earnest (1895) (text)

La Sainte Courtisane and A Florentine Tragedy Fragmentary. First published 1908 in Methuen's Collected Works

(Dates are dates of first performance, which approximate better to the probable date of composition than dates of publication.)

The Importance of Being Earnest and Other Plays. Penguin Classics, 2000. Edited with an Introduction, Commentaries and Notes by Richard Allen Cave. Contains all from above save the first two. Salome is in English.

As an appendix there is one excised scene from The Importance of Being Earnest.

POSTHUMOUS (PREVIOUSLY UNPUBLISHED)

De Profundis (Written 1895-97, in Reading Gaol). Expurgated edition published 1905; suppressed portions 1913, expanded version in The Letters of Oscar Wilde (1962).

The Rise of Historical Criticism (Written while at college) First published in 1905 (Sherwood Press, Hartford, CT) privately printed. Reprinted in Miscellanies, the last volume of the First Collected Edition (1908).

The First Collected Edition (Methuen & Co., 14 volumes) appeared in 1908 and contained many previously unpublished works.

The Second Collected Edition (Methuen & Co., 12 volumes) appeared in installments between 1909–11 and contained several other unpublished works.

The Letters of Oscar Wilde (Written 1868-1900) Published in 1962. Republished as The Complete Letters of Oscar Wilde (2000), with letters discovered since 1962, and new annotations by Merlin Holland.

The Women of Homer (Written 1876, while at college). First published in Oscar Wilde: The Women of Homer (2008) by The Oscar Wilde Society.

The Philosophy of Dress First published in The New-York Tribune (1885), published for the first time in book form in Oscar Wilde On Dress (2013).

MISATTRIBUTED

Teleny, or The Reverse of the Medal (Paris, 1893) has been attributed to Wilde, but its authorship is unclear. One theory is that it was a combined effort by several of Wilde's friends, which he may have edited.

Constance On September 14, 2011, Wilde's grandson Merlin Holland contested Wilde's claimed authorship of this play entitled Constance, scheduled to open that week in the King's Head Theatre. It was not, in fact, "Oscar Wilde's final play," as its producers were claiming. Holland said Wilde did sketch out the play's scenario in 1894, but "never wrote a word" of it, and that "it is dishonest to foist this on the public." The Artistic Director Adam Spreadbury-Maher of the King's Head Theatre and producer of Constance pointed out that Wilde's son, Vyvyan Holland, wrote in 1954, "a significant amount of the dialogue (of Constance) bears the authentic stamp of my father's hand". There is further proof that the developed scenario that Constance was reconstituted from was written by Wilde between 1897 and his death in 1900, rather than the 1894 George Alexander scenario which Merlin Holland quotes.